You've got to start somewhere

By the same author: *How human can you get?*

A comparison of the humanist and Christian views of man's potential
Paperback, 160 pages, IVP

YOU'VE GOT TO START SOMEWHERE
... when you think about education

Charles Martin
Principal of Bilborough Sixth Form College, Nottingham

Inter-Varsity Press

Inter-Varsity Press
38 De Montfort Street, Leicester LE1 7GP, England

© CHARLES MARTIN 1979

All rights reserved. No part of this publication may be reproduced, stored in a retrieval system, or transmitted, in any form or by any means, electronic, mechanical, photocopying, recording or otherwise, without the prior permission of Inter-Varsity Press.

Most of the quotations from the Bible are the author's own paraphrase.

First published 1979

ISBN 0 85110 410 X

Set in 10/11 Baskerville
Typeset by Computacomp (UK) Ltd, Fort William, Scotland
Printed in Great Britain by
William Collins Sons & Co Ltd, Glasgow

Inter-Varsity Press is the publishing division of the Universities and Colleges Christian Fellowship (formerly the Inter-Varsity Fellowship), a student movement linking Christian Unions in universities and colleges throughout the British Isles, and a member movement of the International Fellowship of Evangelical Students. For information about local and national activities in Great Britain write to UCCF, 38 De Montfort Street, Leicester LE1 7GP.

Contents

Preface	7
1. Where do I start?	9
2. Begin at the beginning	17
3. The knowledge market	25
4. Alternatives that are not alternatives	37
5. How to live with the sociology of education	55
6. Psychology for psaints?	75
7. Applications	97
Over to you	127

Preface

This book has arisen out of a discussion group that tried to think in a Christian way about education. It soon became clear that very many teachers and teachers in training were unaccustomed to criticize their educational philosophy (if any) – or what they hear or read – by reference to any specifically Christian principles. Many accepted texts do not make clear the presuppositions upon which they build; some assume a broadly optimistic humanist view of man and society. Christianity, if mentioned at all, is viewed as an optional extra, respectable in moderation, dangerous if taken too seriously, but certainly not basic to the study of education. Students of education, in particular, could easily complete their initial training without realizing any close relations of their Christian belief to the content of their courses.

It seemed necessary, therefore, to focus attention on presuppositions. What do people take for granted? Have Christians anything specific to contribute at this level?

Although I must take responsibility for the book as it is, I must thank the discussion group for their encouragement (even coercion). Thanks are due also to Roger Fielding who provided material for the chapter on sociology. My indebtedness to many, many others who have, over the years, made me think about my trade, is beyond acknowledgment. I only hope that some of their wisdom filters through to the reader. My thanks, also, to Gill Payne for typing the manuscript.

C.G.M.

1. Where do I start?

If you want to build a house, you need foundations. If the foundations are shaky there will soon be cracks in the walls. It's no good saying what a trendy design the house is. It is no better than the foundation it is built on. You could go still further back and, before starting to build, get an expert to make test borings, check the sub-soil and work out what will make the foundations firm enough. If you are really super-cautious you could try and check up on the 'expert'. Has he got the right qualifications? Does he know what he is doing?

Take a different kind of building operation – an Egyptian building a pyramid. The foundation is all right and he's just starting to mark it out. He uses a knotted rope giving a 3–4–5 ratio to get a right angle. If someone says 'Prove it', he could send them across the Mediterranean to see Pythagoras, who would tell them that $3^2 + 4^2 = 5^2$, *QED*. Argument rages on just how Pythagoras got this idea, but the average third-former gets it (or used to get it) from another ancient geometer, Euclid, and his presupposition that 'through a given point, one and only one line can be drawn parallel to a given line.' Those who follow 'modern maths' may have some other intuitively compelling way of proving the 3–4–5 rule. But the friendly Egyptian may not be interested in Euclid's axiom. He might say 'I don't need to bother with all that; my bit of rope works.' That sounds fair enough but in fact creates a king-size philosophical problem: how do you know it works? How do you know you get a right angle? If you have some other way of knowing it is a right angle, why use the 3–4–5 rule in the first place? All very confusing and circular. But Pharaoh says 'Build the pyramid' so the builder tells the wise-guy to get lost, and goes back to his rope.

Starting to teach

What's this got to do with teaching, you say? I'm training to be a teacher, not a philosopher.

Building pyramids is kids' stuff compared to teaching children, and the great trouble is that people who set out to teach children spend so little time sorting out their basic thinking. They are like builders arguing about the colour of the paintwork, but giving no thought to the foundations. Or, to use a different metaphor, it has been said that British educational discussion is like people making a car. They are allowed to discuss everything – engine, styling, trim, colour – but the one question they must *not* ask is 'Where are we going to drive this thing when it's finished?' Colleges and departments of education run courses in the philosophy of education, but these have a poor press, being generally labelled boring, unnecessary, subversive, anti-Christian. But what the critics don't realize is that even to make the criticisms you have to start somewhere. *On what basis* do you pronounce it boring, unnecessary, *etc.*?

How or where do you start thinking about the business of education? Maybe you thought you knew – as one knows most things when one is 16 or 17 – and are now realizing that much of what you took for granted is open to all sorts of challenges. All sorts of questions arise about things that once seemed common sense. And behind the questions come other questions.

For example, why teach Pythagoras to this lot? Why teach Pythagoras at all? Is Pythagoras important? Is it true? How do you find out? And if you don't know the answers to all these questions at once, ought you to be teaching at all?

Or you might start thinking about the customers. Are children likely to be the least interested in Pythagoras? Ought they to be? How do they learn? How will you know if they've *understood* and not just learned another trick? How do you foster understanding? Do schools foster understanding? Is that what schools are for? Who says what schools are for?

Questions behind questions, leading back to very basic matters of value, existence and purpose. The quest is not only for Christians – everyone is making assumptions somewhere along the line. The important thing is to know what the assumptions are. It's no good for an unbeliever to accuse Christians of 'just believing' – he's got to make some assumptions himself somewhere. As Michael Polanyi, himself a professor of physical chemistry, once wrote, a scientist may be afraid he will one day 'catch himself believing', but believe he must, if he is to do any science.

The story so far

People have been thinking about these questions for a long time. Plato, Aristotle & Co. are often regarded as pioneers in the thinking business, but in fact they simply tried to get some system into ideas that had been around for years. People who had to get a living hunting, shooting (bows and arrows) and fishing didn't have much time to put their ideas down, except for the odd cave-painting. But as things became more leisurely (often with the help of a few slaves) there was time to sort it all out, as Socrates is said to have done. He asked awkward questions of everyone and when they gave obvious answers he asked them how they knew and where they based their argument. His admirer, Plato, wrote down (his version of) Socrates' dialogues. Even today they make fascinating reading, not least because they raise so many questions that are still unresolved. His famous paradox (in the *Meno*) is with us still:

If you know the answer to your problem, why do you look for it?

If you don't know the answer to your problem, how will you know it *is* the answer when you find it?

What is it that brings certainty and knowledge into a situation of doubt? What is the learning process? You see the change of expression on the child's face and know he's 'got it', but what does this mean? Plato cleverly illustrates how even a slave could be taught to discover the meaning of the square root of two. What is this grasp of enlightenment? On the other hand, what is it that is grasped – a 'truth' eternally somewhere in space? A convention agreed by those in authority? An impression in the mind?

These questions are likely to crop up here and there in your college lectures – if they don't, stick your own oar in and ask them; they are fundamental to the trade you are taking up.

The Greeks didn't settle it, of course. Discussing knowledge and truth became a respectable pastime whenever war, barbarity or luxury allowed. It got the name philosophy, and Arabs and Chinese had a go at it, as well as Romans and other incipient Europeans. By the 16th century there were enough mutually contradictory writings to fill the budding libraries. Various thinkers tried to put it straight, or start again. If you are doing more than the minimum compulsory philosophical course, you may meet some of them – Descartes, Hume, Locke, Kant, Hegel, Marx, great names all, paving the way for colourful characters of more recent years and the full-time industry of philosphy departments in modern universities. But all, in their different ways, are trying to say where you start. Where is the 'GO' at which you collect your first philosophical £200?

But surely ...

You may well want to protest any time now. Why not

start with 'God says ...'? All this philosophy business is just a smokescreen to cover people's reluctance to accept the plain teaching of Scripture.

That's fine in the close circle of Christian buddies, but is less easy if you try to pass on your belief – especially to people who don't start where you start. 'God says ...' is met with 'Who is God and why should I care what he says?'. Then you begin to have some fellow-feeling for Moses who was brought up sharp by Pharaoh's 'Who is the LORD that I should obey him?' (Ex. 5:22). It is true that Moses did finally see Pharaoh and his hosts dead on the seashore, but you do not really want to see your class engulfed in the nearest sea. You want them to gain some true insight into living in God's world. Where does *their* thinking start, and how do you latch on to it?

You may also have a twinge, when you discover that all through history people who started with 'God says ...' ended up persecuting each other and crusading because they couldn't agree about what God meant by whatever he said. You can always get the pope or caliph to give you a line, but how do you know that's what God really meant?

Another twinge comes when you think about your own start to faith. A few people, perhaps, actually did start with the Bible, but for many there was a chain of other people and events before they got to the Bible. As for your start in other areas of knowledge it's most unlikely you began consciously with God, though perhaps you find him the key to your understanding now.

Choice not chatter

Another, different, reaction arising out of frustration with philosophy is the recent rise of existentialism. You may have met this in your A level French or English literature. If not, here's the gist. Looking for a firm base, they say, is a waste of time. Life is a 'leap'. Nothing is given. You must choose for yourself. You make yourself, and live authentically in what is 'truth for you'. So the jargon goes – and there is truth in it. Christians have been saying for years that you must believe in order to understand; it's no good following conventions; you must believe for yourself if you want 'real life'. But it can't be the whole story. How does the existentialist know? If he says 'nothing is given', is *that* 'given'? If so, how does he know? If all knowledge is subjective, depending upon individual commitment, then he can't tell you anything that is 'true for you', unless he lets his subjectivity slip in an unauthentic moment.

You will meet two opposing standpoints in the arguments and discussions you hear: the empiricist starts with sense-experience, bound by fixed laws of science, so that everything is explained, there is no personal choice or meaning left. If this were true, you could never know it had no meaning.

At the other extreme, the existentialist wants to break out of the strait-jacket of fixed laws or conventions and live by personal decision. If this were the whole truth, then he could never communicate it to others. Neither Shakespeare nor the Beano can give authentic information. Each person must find out for himself.

What happens next?

In the last analysis, when the chips are down, at the end of the day, when the crunch comes, or whatever cliché you use to describe the end of a tiring bit of thinking, you wonder if you've really proved anything. You may even suspect that the Olympian figures who give such fluent lectures (or write such impressive books) are bogged down in the same slough. With centuries of philosophical chat producing so many loose ends, you are going to be smart indeed to get it all tied up. You may feel your training to date has not helped you much. We can't promise this book will, but we hope it will make clear the points from which various people start, and how these starting-points affect the way they look at education. This will have two advantages. First, it is important to understand your own position, where it is based and how it can be argued. You may have several bright ideas about education, and talk about them loud and often. But they will carry more weight if they are clearly related together and to presuppositions that can be plainly spelt out. Secondly, it is important to know other people's positions and to see where you find common cause with them. There will be some parts of teaching where you can work together without any tension at all. In other parts, a difference of presupposition may lead to an unbridgeable gulf between two ways of looking at the world. Christian, Marxist and Hindu may have no difficulty in team-teaching anatomy, but would find it hard to agree on how the information should be set in the context of marriage and the family – and still harder to agree on how to deal with children's questions about how life began at all.

Further back

One final point before we pick a starting-point for this book. We shall argue that Christians start 'further back'. Other views, often true, are in fact deductions from this more basic beginning. If you start 'further back' then you may join forces with your colleague somewhere down the line. But for him the point where you meet may be where *he starts.*

For example, you may share with your humanist colleague a sensitivity to certain literature. You may both be able to lead pupils into a similar understanding of the human condition, the darkness, alienation, aggression or whatever the hero shows. You may discuss the authenticity of the characters who show care, of the hero's fleeting struggle to recall a lost ideal. For you, this may be 'part-way down', stemming from your understanding of the grief and glory that is man, alienated from God yet bearing part of the divine stamp. Your humanist colleague will not follow you 'back'. For him this *is* humanity. Attempts to get behind that 'is' are, for him, the realms of mythology and fantasy, a reluctance to settle for the real world. So what for you is a deduction from a more basic presupposition, is, for him, the starting-point.

2. Begin at the beginning

Where shall we start? Since this book is for Christians who are teaching or training to teach, we shall make God our starting-point. Please read on, at least briefly, while we try to justify so unusual a statement.

It was suggested that we might start with 'a doctrine of man' but that would be (in Christian terms) to start partway down, since man is a created being. You may think starting with God is to assume too much, and we ought to lead folk gently along to a point where they might agree that God is a possibility. That approach would perhaps be appropriate to certain books for certain purposes, but if you are a Christian wanting to teach then presumably at some time you have accepted the Christian position in which God looms large. If you are not a Christian then the shelves are weighed down with books leading you in various degrees of gentleness to look at the evidence.[1] Still you may cringe because, in deep reality, although you are Christian, you are ploughing through doubt and difficulty. What seemed clear and bright at the beginning of your Christian experience now looks something of a cliff-hanger. I'm sorry about that, though it does happen, and not only to fainting Christians who want to be teachers. So there is another shelf weighed down with books to help the doubting Christian.[2] It won't help if this book merely tries to summarize what is said more clearly and lengthily there. But it may help if we can show how starting with God makes sense of education. If someone shows you that petrol will make the car go, it will at least help you from A to B, even if you are unclear about the chemistry of hydrocarbons. It may also, over a ride or two, strengthen the childhood belief that cars were meant to run on petrol – designed that way in fact.

Am human, must believe

That word 'belief' may raise an eyebrow or two, so we must put in a short plea on behalf of faith. Commitment to a presupposition is not a substandard, humanity-degrading wallow, but part of basic human activity. You have to start somewhere. Without making some assumption you can't get off the ground in any area of human thought or action, any more than you can equip a machine-tool factory without starting with some tools. When the writer to Hebrew Christians said 'He who comes to God must believe that he is, and that he rewards those who seek him with diligence' (Heb. 11:6) he was using religious language and talking about the knowledge of God. He could just as well have used scientific language and said 'He who comes to physics must believe there are laws of physics that can be discovered if he looks for them.' The notions of a real world, cause-and-effect, regularity, are things you *bring to* the study of physics, not things you get by looking at experiments. The same could be said of personal relationship: 'He who comes to Bloggs must believe he is a person, who can be chatted up if one tries.' You can't *prove* Bloggs is more than animal, but you can approach him in the belief that he can respond as a person.

All this may be a bit old hat nowadays, but time was when Christian believers were sternly (or even sarcastically) told by some lecturers to forget all the religious stuff and 'be objective', concentrate on the facts and not go in for ideas that could not be 'proved'. Gradually the message is seeping in and more people (even if not Christian) admit you have to start somewhere. They will even be prepared to admit they have a presupposition or two, here and there, among their intellectual baggage. On closer examination some of these may prove to have Christian origins – like the claret which the girl in C. S. Lewis's *Pilgrim's Regress* shyly confessed 'is from Mother Kirk ... anyway, I need it. It is only this keeps me alive.'[3]

So, laying aside our inhibitions, let us admit that we are Christian and start with God and see where that gets us in thinking about education. This will have a number of incidental advantages. It will forearm us against the temptation to think of our Christian faith as something tacked on to the rest of our life – like collecting stamps or taking a friend out for a meal. For too long, too many Christians have kept their Christian belief and their workaday trade in separate compartments.

It will also have the – perhaps surprising – effect of showing us how many of the end-products are the same as those obtained by people who would make no claim to Christian belief. This ought not to be surprising. If the world is God's idea and is meant to run in certain ways, people who try to make it run at all are likely to hit on many of the ways by which it was intended to run. Especially as the equipment to run the show with, which God gave man in the first place, is still available, even to people who won't acknowledge God as the giver. But more of that when we come to the next stage.

What sort of God?

Starting with God sounds nice and simple, but of course leads straight to a demand for more detail. So we must add, with Paul, 'though there are so-called gods both in heaven and earth, gods and lords galore in fact, to us there is only one God, the Father, from whom everything comes and for whom we live' (1 Cor. 8:5,6). It is worth noting that the Bible writers never ask 'Is there God?' but 'What is God like?' 'How do we know what he is like?' 'What ought we to do about it?'. They struggle with language of course, because it is hard to talk about the infinite God in language that comes from finite human experience, but they manage quite well and with much less embarrassment than modern philosophers. Consider some of the characteristics they give.

God as initiator

God does things, has ideas, puts them into effect. He is the beginning, both in the sense that there is no 'before' him, and in the sense that he is the only ultimate power supply there is. He does things because he wants to, not because he has to. In philosophical terms he is necessary, not contingent, being. The classical doctrine of creation *ex nihilo* (out of nothing) tries to say something about this. Julie Andrew's sang 'Nothing comes from nothing ...' and this may be true once things are ticking over in the human realm, but will not do for talk about God. He does not need materials to 'make' with. He creates so that what he creates owes its being to God alone and is entirely dependent upon him. Yet what he creates has objectivity and (as we may see later) can be understood and controlled by those who disbelieve that God created it.

God is one

This is the keynote of the Hebrew confession. 'Yahweh our God, Yahweh is One' (Deut. 6:4). There are no short cuts to dualism. However tough it may be to make sense of good and evil, strife and suffering, you can't shuffle the tricky bits off on to someone else. Ultimately God is one and carries the can. Theodicy is the technical name for attempts to show that God is right even in what seems to be the hard places of evil and suffering. There is a large literature on the subject. But people make the attempt only because they believe that God is one, and cannot shift any blame to anyone else. God's oneness is no solitude or isolation. The doctrine of the Trinity has hit the controversial headlines many times in the history of theology, but is (among other things) an attempt to say that God is social. God relates, loves and shares.

If this seems a far cry and a lot of theology away from

simple statements about 'starting with God' have patience. Any page now we shall try to answer the 'How do you know?' questions, but it won't help us to jump the order.

God is eternal

He doesn't change – although the Bible writers are pushed to find the right language. God doesn't 'repent' or change his mind, they say, but later they tell us that when people turn from wickedness to seek God he changes his attitude and his anger turns to favour. What they are trying to make clear is that God can be relied on. His title I AM sums up, in a never-changing present tense, a person who neither becomes nor fades, neither develops nor declines. Even the dramatic events of the incarnation and Easter, which form a watershed for all history, are only the projections on the screen of space and time of the 'eternal purpose' – that great love which like a fire is *always* burning in *his* heart.

God communicates

The next two characteristics of God are difficult to separate. They are, in fact, particular cases of God as initiator. God may have other irons in the fire than the particular cosmos we know a little about. Creating 'our' universe did not exhaust God any more than writing *King Lear* finished Shakespeare's creative output. But certainly one example of God's initiating that we do know something about is the universe we live in and the people we are. The images used are of God as light and God as giver. 'The light shines in the darkness, and the darkness has not overcome it' (Jn. 1:5). The light is a symbol of communication. The giving is a sign of communication. If the lady finds boxes of chocolates appearing all over the house, she may well think someone is trying to get a message across to her. This is part of God's character. He does not want to keep himself to himself. He goes out in declaration and gift. As the Scouse version of John 1.1 puts it: 'Right from the start, God had summat to say.' One of the ways of 'saying' was to create a world and to people it. For the time being forget evolutionary squabbles. What is important at the moment is that the whole show was God's idea and he carried it out. Just how he carried it out we can perhaps work out later. We may be able to find out from the world around us – in the same way that you could find out a lot about how a radio was made by looking at it and doing tests on it. But for the moment, Creation is God saying and giving. The dual characteristics can be seen in the Psalms: 'The heavens declare the glory of God ...' (Ps. 19:1) and '... the earth hath he given to the children of men.' (Ps. 115:16) – declaration and gift. Romans 1 tells a similar story, though taking account of the twist in man's thinking since he decided to go it alone. Romans 2 goes on to talk of God's continued giving so that men have the ability to understand and know, even if they *are* trying to go it alone – they have 'the law written in their hearts'. There is much more about God communicating, telling and giving, in word and action, history and prophecy, and finally 'in a Son' (Heb. 1:2, *en huiō*).

This hints at the answer to the question 'How do you know?' The simple 'starting with God' has turned out to be a powerfully loaded presupposition. No wonder those who don't start with God accuse Christians of having a metaphysical portmanteau in God from which they can produce whatever argument demands. But it is no good kidding ourselves and pretending that God makes little difference to the way we look at the world. We may not be very good at recognizing the difference; we may not like the difference when we recognize it, since it brings painful obligations and decisions. If at some stage in your life you have committed yourself to belief in God through Christ, you may not grasp quite how far-reaching this can be, but making a firm and unashamed start there may help in at least two ways.

First, it may jerk you sharply, if painfully, into realizing that Christianity claims to have something positive to say. God is light (1 Jn. 1:5). In Christ there are hid all the treasures of wisdom and knowledge (Col. 2:3). Secondly, it may set you thinking about your relationship with others who do not share your own commitment. Your obligation to them is not only to confront them evangelistically with the claims of Christ and the need of their undying souls; you are not only in a position of confrontation, us–them, godly–godless. You are also in a position of sharing. Peter got the right line with Cornelius: 'I also am a man' (Acts 10:26). Since (on your presuppositions) both you and they live in God's world and draw your being continually from God, you will share many experiences with them. You may well think your commitment gives you a framework that makes more sense of those experiences, as well as the power to respond more appropriately. But in many cases you may be surprised to find how much there is to agree about without temporarily suspending your Christian conviction.

Before we look further at the 'How do you know?' question, it is only fair to point out an odd twist that argument takes at this stage in many of those brilliant nocturnal discussions that characterize student life. Christian participants readily assume they are backs-to-the-wall in a desperate situation when asked 'How do you know?'. Admittedly it is a perplexing philosophical question. It is, incidentally, one to which the Bible gives little space. The writers' motto there seems to be 'Carry on knowing' rather than 'Epistemology rules, OK.' But the odd thing is that Christians so rarely rally and ask the enquirers how *they* know. Yet there is no shortage of spade work in this area. Epistemology (the study of knowledge and its sources and how you know it) has been a major industry for centuries but still we are not much further forward than Archimedes with his 'Give me a place to stand …'. Even the chap who wants to throw stones must have somewhere to stand while he throws, and also at least implicit trust in Newtonian physics. Into a dark world the Christian claims to bring the Light of God in the face of Jesus Christ. The light shows up the human situation in all its hope and sorrow. If unbelievers dispute the picture, can they produce lamps of their own? What can they produce as a means of showing any other picture is right? Back to the 3–4–5 rule and Meno's paradox. For Christians to put their lights under bushels is no service in a dark world. For the rest, the words of Jesus are a warning: 'If the light that is in you is darkness, how great is *that* darkness' (Mt. 6:23).

First of all we shall look briefly at a possible Christian epistemology and then at how people in general come to know.

1 *E.g.* J. R. W. Stott, *Basic Christianity* (IVP, 1958).
   Gordon Bridger, *A day that changed the world* (IVP, 1975).
   David Watson, *In search of God* (Falcon, 1974).
   Colin Chapman, *Christianity on trial* (Lion Publishing, 1974).
2 *E.g.* R. Forster and P. Marston, *That's a Good Question* (Coverdale, 1977).
   Os Guinness, *Doubt* (Lion Publishing, 1976).
   D. M. MacKay, *The clockwork image* (IVP, 1974).
   L. Newbigin, *Honest Religion for Secular Man* (SCM Press, 1966).
3 C. S. Lewis, *Pilgrim's Regress* (Geoffrey Bles, 1943, Fontana, 1977).

3. The knowledge market

Knowledge is a tricky commodity to deal in. Or, to use another metaphor, it is a difficult territory to map. On one boundary it merges into instinct, with the word 'know' doing a double act. The new baby instinctively 'knows' how to feed, cry and kick. It soon begins to 'know' from experience that if baby cries Mum comes and picks baby up. Somewhere between then and the time you meet him in the infants' reception class he has collected a pile of knowledge. In some extreme views there is *no* hazy boundary between knowing and instinct – they are both parts of one misunderstood country. Keeping coat and scarf on the right peg is as much the result of conditioning as feeding is; life is literally a rat-race except that humans learn different mazes. There are quite a few books that criticize this strictly behaviourist, deterministic view,[1] so we need only comment that there *is* a 'machine' view of learning, memory and response. It is possible – and some would say desirable – to use rote-learning or some similar technique so that everyone can say the seven-times table and decline *mensa*. Certain motor skills can be imparted in the same way. But there is more to knowledge than patterns on memory cells.

You can think of knowledge as bits of information you collect and file away; and this leads to a consideration of curriculum. What bits are needed? How can the child collect them? How are they to be categorized and filed away? You can also think of knowledge as a mysterious dynamic event. The bits of information won't stay discrete like fragments in a kaleidoscope. Either singly or in combination they appear before the apprehension. Knowledge is an awareness, a personal involvement with some experience, memory, information, some idea or relationship. The units of information are not just in the filing cabinet but present to the consciousness of the knower.

Getting it there

There is another confusion. Knowledge is not only twofold in character – the information filed away, and the awareness. Knowing also includes the business of coming to know, the process involved in getting the bits of information in the filing cabinet at all. In educational terms this process of coming to know might be what we call learning, but that is not all. We don't use 'learning' for 'coming to know' people. The school report which speaks of George 'deepening his knowledge' is not the same as 'learning lots of things'.

The machine view, of course, is in no difficulty here. Information gets lodged in the mind in much the same way as computer storage cores get charged with information. Sense data bombards George and some of it gets stored away in George's memory where much of it will fade exponentially unless kept alive by some system of recall. But the problem of epistemology is not so easily solved. Crucial experiments are hard to conduct, and such evidence as we have leaves some big question-marks over the simple memory-store analogy.

Michael Polanyi has devoted a great deal of work to studying how we come to know, how we fit together the various clues that lead to recognition, how we 'see' connections between similar experiences or relations between ideas in argument. What emerges is no simple stimulus-response mechanism, no filing-cabinet idea of the mind, but a dynamic process aptly summed up in the title of his longest book, *Personal Knowledge*. He criticizes the empiricist (filing-cabinet) view and pleads for *understanding* to be included in a right description of knowledge.

> 'Our acknowledgement of understanding as a valid form of knowing will go a long way towards liberating our minds from this violent and inefficient despotism' (of empiricism).[2]

J. MacMurray makes the distinction between knowledge and information:

> 'Knowledge is always personal, always somebody's; but information is just anybody's. Science wants facts, atoms of information, which must be all indifferent to their being known ...; it is information, the raw material out of which you and I can pick and choose what we want for our purposes, to build up our own knowledge, which is real knowledge just because it is ours and nobody else's.'[3]

Bronowski and Mazlish put it even more strongly:

> 'The participation of the knower in shaping his knowledge which had hitherto been tolerated only as a flaw – a shortcoming to be eliminated from perfect knowledge – is now recognised as the true guide and master of our cognitive powers.'[4]

So education lectures may include material about this elusive 'understanding'. You can condition children to repeat tables or spelling or poetry. You soon find it is a different matter to give understanding of multiplication in terms of areas, sets, or continued addition, or to find meaning in the poetry.

Christian knowledge?

So far the mystery – and muddle – can be understood by people of all faiths or none. This itself is significant. Unbelievers realize, too, that knowing is not information storage. Does Christianity add anything to this? Is 'add' the right word? How should the Christian world-view relate to this business of what is known, the act of knowing, coming to know, the state of knowing?

A Christian can push the mystery back a little further. If man is created in the image of God, then we might ask if the human capacity to know does in some way reflect a similar activity of God. The Bible talks repeatedly about God knowing. In the great majority of cases the word has overtones of assessment, value and judgment. It is never simply the filing of bits of information. Rather is it 'information in the context of relationship'. God is not a cosmic computer eternally printing out or storing information. Certainly he is the one 'to whom all hearts are open, all desires known, and from whom no secrets are hid' but this is an active process of relationship with those he knows, not just filling up record cards.

This would give a clue to man as a knowing subject. He is not merely an animal, programmed with instincts and stimulus-response patterns. In fact, according to Genesis 1 and 2 and Psalm 8, it is precisely because he is in God's image that he has dominion and control over the animal kingdom. He has been given capacities similar in kind to those ascribed to God. His knowing is a dynamic process; it has evaluative overtones. He can reflect, recalling past experience, reviewing, judging, rejoicing. He can look forward and arrange possibilities and make decisions. Because man is limited by time, there has to be, in his experience, a 'coming to know'. No such coming to know is ascribed to God (though it *is* appropriately used of Jesus during his life in Palestine). Some commentators detect a basic difference in the two Greek words used (*ginōskō* and *oida*) suggesting that the first refers to knowledge acquired by learning while the second is intuitive knowledge. Some passages support this distinction and where they are both used in one passage the distinction may be valid, but clear division of meaning cannot be made in all uses. Certainly 'coming to know' is part of normal human experience –

and one of the principal *raisons d'etre* of schools.

Revelation

Central to the biblical ideas of man's knowledge is the concept of God's revelation. Man's finding out is the obverse of God's showing. God is the great initiator. He communicates, in declaration and gift. Romans 1 and 2 refer to both the creation men *experience* (1:19) and the creation men *are*, with 'the law written in the heart' (2:15). Man's capacity to perceive matches God's character as revealer. To use a radio metaphor, it could be said that the frequency band matches. God gets through on various channels and man is equipped to receive on them all – all kinds of experience, external and internal can be processed to yield knowledge. The system breaks down only when a man 'by his wickedness suppresses the truth' (1:18).

But that is not all there is to be said on the matter. The Bible is concerned with questions of why, who and what rather than questions of how. The writers are happy to ascribe the revelatory process to God, to declare *why* he does so and to explain *what* he reveals. They do not say much about the mechanics of the process, *how* it happens. In both Old and New Testaments, there are instances of the Spirit (*ruach*, *pneuma*) of God coming upon people to give them particular insights and abilities. In the New Testament a fresh dimension is added with the *indwelling* of the Holy Spirit by whose anointing 'you all know'. But even in these special endowments there is no explanation of the psychological goings-on, only of the meaning and response. If these are in some way special channels of communication open to those who are consciously in touch with God, how are they related to the ways in which others come to know? There is clearly no warrant for a belief that Christians can be so indwelt by the Spirit that they 'know' the answers to exam questions without the bother of reading books or listening to lectures (even if these are the work of unbelievers).

So a Christian epistemology might make the general statements that knowledge is God's gift; that it links man to reality so that he thinks God's thoughts after him, and gains a true understanding of himself and the world. It would then have to go on to consider the mechanics of this 'coming to know' and in so doing would perhaps find much in common with other analyses. In a similar way, a Christian view of science would begin with God as creator, a source of intelligent energy whose ways can be understood by those who (being made in his image) match or mesh with the intelligence of the creator. From there the journey would be through experiment, hypothesis and deduction, falsification and so on. A theory of entropy or evolution might be developed in this framework as showing how God went about the business of getting the world going and keeping it going. The Christian might well feel he was able to answer some questions from a more helpful viewpoint – e.g., there seems little *evolutionary* use in 'a sense of wonder' or caring for the weak. Also Christians could argue that their view of creation gives them knowledge and insight that lead to a response of thankfulness and joy that is not open in the same way to unbelievers.

Applied to education, the Christian view would hold that all human learning was the correlate of God's revelation. Knowledge is part of God's giving and the mental equipment by which experience is processed and known is God's continual giving. But there will still be work to be done on learning theory, concept-formation, the stages of development and so forth. There will be scope for techniques of sociology to investigate how various social structures and relationships foster or hinder learning, personality development or confidence. Again, there are value judgments associated with these questions and it is difficult to separate hard information (true for Christians and non-Christians) from evaluation where different views of the world will yield widely different priorities.

Package deal

Round about here, Christians will begin to realize how much they are out on a limb with their 'God' presupposition. Later we shall try to see what those who do not have this presupposition might be able to do. They, too, have to start somewhere – experience, history, logic, axiom or hunch. The Christian may have started at any of these points in his quest for faith – or he may, more likely, have heard some declaration of God's salvation and believed it. There followed a process which in God-talk is 'growing up in Christ' or 'renewal of the mind', and from a human point of view is 'fides quaerens intellectum' (faith seeking reason). So he has now arrived at a more or less integrated Christian world-view. He may even be a little embarrassed, on reflection, to find how much he draws from his world-view rather than the 'reasoning' with which he defends his views to others. For example he may realize that the real, inward, reason why he feels that individual children matter is because he understands God's care and love for them, not because of a Kantian doctrine of a kingdom of ends. Other matters are fitted into a value system which is firmly related to biblical teaching. Events are seen in a framework of history which is his story. The Christian has soaked up the biblical view of God's acts interpreted by God's words.

If you try to pass this on to unbelievers you realize they don't have the same framework. It can be quite a shock, which often gives rise to one or other of two equally unhappy outcomes. One is to slate the other chap and tell him roundly that, since he is so blind as not to see the truth, he will never get anything right. The other is to hope you can keep your own framework for Sunday use, and carry on with a different one in everyday work. A more sober reaction is to recognize firmly that you have a light and a chart which will help you find *your* way, and give you a true view of yourself and the world. Others may arrive at partial understanding, which in so far as it is true

31

will agree with the landscape as the light reveals it. So you will expect considerable areas of agreement, or near agreement, but considerable areas where you see more meaning, greater duty, richer cause for thankfulness. It is as though God runs a factory from which each may take what he will. You have done a package deal, taking a machine, maker's phone number, technical adviser and handbook in one huge transaction. You may not always study the handbook properly, or watch the technical adviser closely enough, but it's all yours. Others may just grab a machine and do the best they can with it on their own. There are various extracts from handbooks lying round, culled from previous users, and many more or less successfully operating machines to be looked at, so they can learn a lot if they try.

It may seem big-headed to say you have an advantage over the unbeliever – he, poor chap, must muddle along as best he may. Many such will retort that they seem to get along better than many Christian 'experts'. But there is no escaping the fact that Christianity does claim to bring more light and power into the situation. Potentially at least, comparing like circumstances with like, a Christian has opportunity to see more meaning and to respond more fully to life in the present – and certainly in the future. We shall say more about this when we consider 'alternatives'.

How then?

We have said the Bible does not give many details about how we come to know. But something at least can be derived from the idea of man made in the image of God. The image is spoiled but not shattered entirely, and at any rate it is partly restored and refurbished by relationship with Christ. Two parts of that image may help in thinking about epistemology.

In the first place, God is *one*. There is no dualism, no contradiction. So man, although fallen, strives for the unity he longs to be. Salvation means wholeness (the underlying meaning can be seen, for example, in Luke 7:50; 8:12,36,48,50, where 'saved', 'healed', 'made well' all translate the same Greek word, *sōzō*). Even in our imperfect state we appreciate a principle of cohesion, a sense of antithesis, a refusal to live with intellectual or any other muddle. Experience must make sense. Things that are different cannot be treated as if they were the same. Logicians may think of Aristotle's law of the excluded middle, or Kant's universalist maxim. Others may think of common sense. Eight-year-olds will say, 'It's not fair'. All show some reflection of God who is one. Consistency is not a schoolmaster's foible, but built into man's consciousness. You can suppress it while you do your own private fiddle, but sooner or later it will crop up and you find yourself condemning other people for not being fair to you. Whatever rubbish you churn out in your own arguments, you will jump triumphantly upon a contradiction in your opponent's case. So part of 'coming to know' is filtering experience through a sieve of consistency, cohesion and pattern. We are born jig-saw puzzle solvers. We look for 'fit' and we recognize 'fit' when we see it. We live with *Meno's* paradox and we solve it every day. We feebly reflect God in whose image we are made and in whom there is no variableness nor shadow of turning.

Secondly, we share in the divine characteristics of purpose and initiative. He did not create without purpose. We do not live long in purposelessness. Whatever we say about life being meaningless; whatever high-sounding existentialist jargon we adopt about the absurd; whatever our late-night discussions say about man rootless and rudderless; when morning comes we find ourselves setting off to get somewhere – to a bank to cash a cheque, to a garage to buy petrol, to a travel agent to book a holiday. We have a built-in respect for purpose. We expect things not only to make sense, but to be aimed somewhere. Not only must they be caused *by* something, but *for* something. So we are set upon enquiry. We do not sit tight waiting for everything to come to us. We take the initiative of discovery. We map out a plan of action. Whether in the sand-pit in the primary school, or in Nuffield physics, we 'come to know' by initiative, looking, handling, trying. This is all with an underlying expectation that there is something to find out, some unifying idea that will explain the individual experiences, some purpose that will satisfy our longing to know why. As Polanyi says,[5] we are a company of explorers. He makes a distinction between explicit and tacit knowledge and points out that we are always attending *from* and attending *to*. We pay attention *to* experience, taking the initiative, questing, seeking. But we do so because tacitly our attention is *from* a firm base of expectancy. We listen carefully to the unfamiliar accents of a Tyneside acquaintance, expecting him to be making sense in a variant of a language we recognize. If it were not for this underlying, unspoken expectation *from* which we pay attention, there would be no point in listening *to* him at all. However sceptical we try to be, curiosity overpowers us. We are a company of explorers even when we deny there is anything to discover. Even people who deny there is any God to discover spend their lives trying to find out what happens on Mars, or the location of the next black hole in space.

Since we are developing people – and children are people-in-the-making, not mini-adults – these two qualities of God don't appear fully fledged. Quite apart from the facts of human sinfulness and rebellion, we are not eternal and so we build up our experience block by block. We may (according to Jung) start with a stock of archetypes, or (according to Kant) a couple of mental filing cabinets, but we are only slowly building up the stock of experience on which we use this equipment. Yet still the fact is that we recognize inconsistency when we see it; we may well try to put it right. And we do not stay purposeless for long, or at least not without saying how boring it is. Humanity is not infinitely plastic. It has certain built-in tendencies, just as the run of the ground determines which way the rain water will flow. We could just conceivably play rugby with marbles, but we could hardly play tiddleywinks. So the human equipment seems suited for some variant of the game 'Go and look for meaning.' It does not lend itself to playing at being cogs in a machine or flotsam at sea. Christians think this is because God designed us that way. Other people can account for it how they like, but in practice usually act as if they (and the children they teach) can take the initiative and recognize truth when they discover it.

1 M. A. Jeeves, *Psychology and Christianity: the view both ways* (IVP, 1976).
   D. M. MacKay, *The clockwork image* (IVP, 1974).
2 M. Polanyi, *Personal Knowledge* (Routledge & Kegan Paul, 1958).
3 J. MacMurray, *Reason and Emotion* (Faber, 1962).
4 J. Bronowski and B. Mazlish, *The Western Intellectual Tradition* (Penguin, 1963).
5 M. Polanyi, *The Tacit Dimension* (Routledge & Kegan Paul, 1967).

4. Alternatives that are not alternatives

The paradoxical title comes from Galatians 1:6,7, where Paul berates 'another gospel which is not another'. He uses two Greek words: first 'a different one' (*heteros*); secondly 'an alternative' (*allos*). The rival gospel was certainly 'different' from what he had preached to the Galatians. But they must beware of thinking of it as an alternative. It was not the same sort of thing. In spite of similarities, it could not do the same job. So, in starting on the educational trek, there are a number of other starting-points. Once again you may be embarrassed to find that Christian allegiance makes you seem a bit big-headed, because you have to say that some of these other starting-points are 'heteros' – they just won't do the job. They don't give a firm basis to build on. They don't account for children as we meet them or knowledge as we understand it. Some are very helpful and you can go along with them, but then you realize that they are included somewhere in the fuller Christian picture we looked at before.

Don't go mad over this, making enemies and influencing people against you by telling them how useless their starting-points are. Be thankful that they go to the bother of trying to set out a stall. At least that is what you would expect from what *you* know of man made in the image of God. The fact that anyone tries to make a consistent case, to knock some order into things and show what it's all aimed at, is a good sign. It shows he's human. Sheep and caterpillars take the landscape as they find it and make their way round the obstacles. Men go in for map-making and town and country planning. So give him the good news first – glad to see you're trying to make sense of everything. That makes two of us. As Peter said, 'I also am a man'. (Acts 10:26) But that doesn't stop you having antennae twitching to pick out the starting-points that are bogus.

When you look at the starting-points that have been proposed, you find that almost all of them have latched on to something true about human nature. Sometimes they make it *the* thing; then it gets out of proportion and so obscures other views. In education each starting-point may be useful, though you will have to watch that one perfectly proper view of the child does not make a take-over bid and turn the poor child into a lop-sided freak.

Seven truths about mankind

There are, of course, more than seven different schemes of thought, each with its own presupposition or starting-point. The seven chosen for comment are not entirely distinct, but represent viewpoints that crop up frequently in general discussion and in educational thinking. People don't always live consistently with one, but hop about from one to the other. This hopping about is itself valuable; it shows that each of the seven represents a true insight into human nature – and it ought to warn the hoppers that their professed aim is not the only one and cannot make a take-over bid for the whole of human life.

1. *Man is a machine*

(Have clockwork – will tick) The scientific method has been so successful in finding out how things work that, not surprisingly, people have looked at *men* scientifically to find out how *they* work. They have made good progress at finding out how all the physical bits and pieces work – nerves, cells, DNA, blood, hormones, how diseases are caused and countered – and naturally press on to enquire how thought, emotion, action are caused. You have probably heard of Pavlov and his dogs and how he conditioned them to respond to various stimuli. Other researchers have experimented with rats. It seemed logical enough to apply the results to human beings. Brainwashing is an extreme example of such application; advertising a less painful one. All seem to show that we *are* just machines who respond to stimuli like computers responding to the instructions typed on the terminal. The deepest conditioning force of all, according to sociobiologist Edward Wilson,[1] is the urge for survival of our genes. Even altruistic action can be explained (says Wilson) as the selfish gene looking after its offspring. At less spectacular levels every teacher expects teaching method to influence learning. Children do respond to stimuli in predictable ways. Memory appears to be built up by reinforcement and recall. For some purposes at least we *are* machines; rather less reliable than tape-recorders, but capable of similar response.

The trouble comes when this view is claimed to be all there is. Man is 'really only' a machine. This is an example of the fallacy of reductionism, reducing a complex situation to a deceptively simple account. In effect this treats one account as the only possible account and takes one viewpoint as the only viewpoint. Taken to extremes – as by some sociobiologists – it disposes of all choice or self-determination, all goodwill or evil intent. Freud's psychology has a strong mechanistic base – there is little account of free choice, decision or personal feeling. Eysenck and B. F. Skinner are names you will meet in the psychology of learning. Durkheim and Marx show similar tendencies in analysing society. For everything there is a 'scientific' cause. Value, morality and God are inventions brought about by economic or social pressures on people.

One famous implication of this position is the so-called naturalistic fallacy, the attempt to establish what 'ought' to be from what 'is'. According to this view, morals are derived from *mores* (the custom), *i.e.*, from what people do rather than what people ought to do.

Any sentence involving 'ought' has to be translated into a form involving 'is'; no judgment, praise or blame, is possible, only a description. So 'right' becomes 'socially acceptable', 'wrong-doing' becomes 'deviance'. For some purposes, the 'machine' view is a useful way to understanding. Professor Donald MacKay points out the dangers:

> 'Let me say at once that my own research department at Keele is concerned with the mechanisms of the brain, and that our working hypothesis is that the brain is capable of being studied as a mechanistic system. In order to explain human behaviour, chains of cause and effect can legitimately be sought and found in terms of physics, or physiology, or at still higher levels in terms of information-engineering or psychology. The last thing I want to suggest is that there is anything improper about a mechanistic approach as such. What I do want to emphasize, however, is that a mechanistic approach adopted for scientific purposes is being abused if it leads to what I am calling machine-mindedness. There is all the difference in the world between describing and analysing a particular system as a mechanism, and claiming that the "real" explanation, the only worthwhile or objective explanation to be had of the situation, is the explanation you get in terms of machine analogies.'[2]

2. *Man is a bundle of appetites*

(Have senses – will enjoy) This is a form of the 'machine' theory, only now it is not just a machine like a clock with wheels turning remorselessly and unfeelingly on. Man is a *feeling* machine. He feels what is happening; he experiences pain, fear, curiosity, hunger, sexual desire, excitement, aggression. This is the view popularized by Desmond Morris in his *The Naked Ape*.[3] Men are 'really only' animals. Reductionism again. All discussion of morality, value, duty or religion is cut out. They are quickly reduced to some expression of fear or aggression or (for the popular press) sexual fantasy. Applied to criminology it means you treat the patient, rather than punish the offender. Applied to education, you train the animal rather than teach the person. It is a despairing view of man, which shows through much recent literature. All the things that are lovely, honourable, worthy of praise, that Paul tells us to fill our minds with, are scraped away as a thin veneer of culture to reveal the 'reality' of the animal underneath, cowering in fear, teeth bared in self-defence, or breaking out of frustrated desire. One by one the achievements which have been celebrated in art, music, literature and religion are taken apart and reduced to a sorry, bedraggled pile of instincts and undeniable urges.

As before, of course, there is truth in it. We *are* animals. The hungers, drives and aggressions that children (and adults) feel are real factors in living and learning. But they are not the only factors. *Naked Ape or Homo Sapiens* by Lewis and Towers[4] is a useful rejoinder if you can get hold of it, particularly as one author is Christian and the other not. Neither is happy with the 'only animal' description of man.

3. *Man is a social animal*

(Have companions – will live together) This follows as a more refined version of the previous viewpoint. Most animals have some form of social or group relations. These can be explained simply as instincts, helping the group survive, as Konrad Lorenz investigated in his greylag geese, or Desmond Morris in *The Naked Ape*. Sociologists tend to use terms that are more human (in the sense that they do not use these terms of animal experiments). Words like 'self-image', 'relationship', 'pleasure', 'approval' are some way on from basic drives like hunger and survival.

In traditional ethical terms this section includes several old friends. Hedonism (the view that the motivation for human behaviour is pleasure – Greek *hedone* = pleasure) is still alive and kicking even among those who wouldn't know its technical name. It comes in at least two varieties. Psychological hedonism says that pleasure *is* the stimulus for behaviour, and therefore is a variant of the first or second truth above. This version leads to the 'stick and carrot' attitude which many teachers adopt in practice. They can claim ancient patronage for their attitude since Aristotle shared it. Some people can work things out, he thought, but with 'artisans and mechanics' who couldn't understand moral reasoning you had to resort to rewards and punishments. In that remote 4th century BC no-one seems to have used the Greek equivalent of 'manipulating' for his suggested programme.

The other version, ethical hedonism, says that pleasure *ought to be* the motive for behaviour. One man's overzealous search for *his* pleasure will be offset by another man's efforts to avoid displeasure or pain. This was developed by such thinkers as Jeremy Bentham and John Stuart Mill to embrace everyone and urge the 'greatest good of the greatest number' (they assumed 'good' = 'pleasure'). Mill attempted to refine this with his 'hedonistic calculus' showing how you weighed one pleasure against another; and also with the so-called 'hedonistic paradox'. According to this latter you obtain pleasure incidentally, as you aim for other goals, such as the common good. If you aim just for pleasure, you will probably miss it. But the motivation is the same – other things may be followed *because* they lead to pleasure all round.

This development, usually known as utilitarianism, underlies much of our present society's attitude to life and behaviour, and therefore to education. The job of the state is seen as providing a framework in which each can enjoy himself without causing pain to others. 'I like it, what harm is there in it?' is the distillation of man-in-the-street ethics. So education must show children how to live together, weighing pleasure and pain for themselves and others. The reductionism slips in when *everything* has to be explained in terms of the search for pleasure; when all love and duty is reduced to a calculation of 'what I get out of it' or 'what other people like'. We are social animals, it is true, so hedonists and utilitarians make a good point. But it is not the only point.

4. *Intuition*

(Have hunches – will catch on) Whether they bring pleasure or pain, some actions just seem right. The intuition lobby majors on the persistent impression that human beings know what they ought to do. The strongest traditional expression of this is in the idea of conscience, which has always been viewed as something built in to mankind, a feeling in the bones, a moral compass. It is usually regarded as being roughly the same for everyone – 'you know better than that'; 'everyone knows ...'; 'any fool can see ...'. Although this view cannot go it alone, it has a great deal of truth in it. Michael Polanyi was mentioned just now, and he is one of many who have emphasized the human capacity to 'recognize sense', to grasp meaning, in every area of human enquiry. Difficulties appear when people's hunches lead them to different ideas about the same thing. Classroom howlers usually refer to children catching on to the wrong thing, following the wrong clue, and such hunches are remarkably resistant to teachers' efforts to show why they are wrong. At the level of values, intuition has always been in rough weather because of the differing values which differing people hold 'in good conscience'. Sociologists are quick to point out how 'conscience' depends upon upbringing; psychologists give an account of its origin in the 'crisis of infancy'. Yet still it exercises a mysterious power over us, and we have (as J. H. Jacques points out in *The Right and the Wrong*[5]) 'to account for our fundamental moral convictions'. The objection that conscience gives so many divergent deliverances as to make it useless has been countered robustly by C. S. Lewis (*Abolition of Man*[6]) and Ginsberg (*Diversity of Morals*[7]). One Christian, one not, both show there is an impressive body of geographically and historically agreed principle among mankind.

Intuition is closely bound up with the notion of natural law, where it overlaps with the next section. The idea that mankind knows 'by nature' that he is morally responsible has biblical warrant (Rom. 2:14ff.) and was the accepted wisdom of the middle ages. It is still powerfully developed by orthodox Roman Catholicism.

5. *Man is rational*

(Have brains – will work it out) This is one of the oldest trademarks in the knowledge business. Aristotle, as we have seen, thought your average workie would have to be kept going with punishment or reward, but he was sure the top people could 'work it out' and decide by reason how their society should be run and how they should behave. 'Practical wisdom is a rational faculty exercised for the attainment of truth in things that are humanly good and bad.' Before him, Plato had given a cogent analysis of *forms* (or *ideas*) of which particular things and actions were instances. Behind these lay the idea or form of the 'good' which illuminated all, as the sun illuminated all natural objects. Reason was the instrument by which man grasped these ideas. His mind was illuminated 'like a light caught from a leaping flame', and he was able to apply these guiding ideas to all situations. A great 18th century name in the defence of reason is Immanuel Kant. His two major works, *Critique of Pure Reason* and *Critique of Practical Reason*, set out a detailed system of how the rational mind processes experience to yield a coherent picture, firstly of the world as an exact machine, governed by rules of cause-and-effect, and, secondly, of the world as the place of man's moral endeavour where 'ought implies can' and he is free to know and do what is morally right. Kant did not suffer fools gladly and his system is rigorous and hard; so not surprisingly it slid from popular favour. His insistence that people could reason their way to truth, a universal truth that was inevitably true for every rational person, did not go down well with folk who liked a bit of variety and permission to 'think their own thing'. It ran into difficulty, too, with people who were not very good at thinking, and still today the most ardent Kantian will agree that the least able children who find moral reasoning difficult may have to be helped with a firm framework of guidance and direction because they *can't* work it out for themselves.

Kant's ideas – or perhaps it would be truer to say, the idea of reason as the basic human distinctive quality – have staged a come-back recently. John Wilson (*Introduction to Moral Education*[8]) gave a rational review of the task in moral education. A right action, in moral terms, is 'done for a reason, the right reason, understood to be the right reason, because it is the right reason' as a result of a belief which the actor wishes to be universally valid and prescriptive.

The 'reason' approach has been applied to education in general in the well-known work of Peters and Hirst (*Logic of Education*[9]) and Hirst (*Moral Education in a Secular Society*[10]) with the emphasis upon 'forms of knowledge'. People, and specially children, come to knowledge – as opposed to habit, convention, hunch or any other 'irrational way of acting' – by building up a series of rational networks going back to basic ideas which are not themselves open to question (as, *e.g.*, it is senseless to ask 'What is the reason for having reasons?'). This educational philosophy has been challenged sharply, particularly by some Christian writers who claim it does not take enough account of man's reason being impaired by the Fall. It is, however, very nimbly defended, and (quite properly) a widely used way of provoking students to think about the knowledge trade they have joined. Trouble only comes when this system makes a take-over bid as the *only* place to start. Any attempt at such a take-over bid soon begins to show up the strains as 'reason' has to take in more and more parts of personality. From being pure intellectual activity, it soon spreads to cover activities which any self-respecting intuitionist would claim for conscience, or innate grasp of value.

6. *Man is a bounding leap*

(Have freedom – will decide) In stark contrast to the fixity of the rational approach, with its insistence on objective reality, true for every rational person, is the existentialist mood. Here, you do not start from some given essence which you can arrive at by rational deduction. Existence is before essence. Existence is the 'act by which I am'. I am free to act, whether I like it or not (and most people don't like it and so retreat into living by convention). So, by my decision and actions, I make myself and arrive at 'truth for me'. It is fair to say that this viewpoint is rarely presented as the one and only starting-point. It usually goes along with a readiness to accept *some* things, like physical properties of matter. Sticks, stones and stars have their fixed properties (might even be allowed as 'essence'), but man is not to be so described and limited. He is 'condemned to be free' and must not retreat into the unworthy and unauthentic living by custom. 'The crowd is the lie'. True living comes by decision.

Clearly there is a lot here that is true. Christians especially have been advocating decision for centuries. You must commit yourself. Believe and know. But they have always insisted that there *are* the right things to know. God's being, as creator, is very much 'given'. So is man's nature as made in God's image but spoiled by sin. As a protest against the sterility of intellectualism or the manipulation of social conditioning, existentialism is a welcome voice in the philosophical wilderness. But as the only point of departure, it fails.

An illustration of both the value and the failure of the approach comes from the way existentialism first hit the English religious headlines with John Robinson's *Honest to God*.[11] Robinson drew heavily on an American, Joseph Fletcher (see his *Situation Ethics*[12]), whose hero is the American cabbie who said: 'There are times when you have to put your principles aside and do the right thing.' So Robinson had a section entitled 'Nothing prescribed – except love.' Have love – will do the caring thing. This was valuable in showing up how legalistic and conventional a lot of Christian morality had become. Far from springing from love, much of it sprang from 'what we always do' and 'what the neighbours think'. The difficulties arose when anyone enquired what *was* the loving thing. Christians (like Augustine, whose celebrated 'Love, and do what you will' hit the headlines at this time) meant God's love, shed abroad in our hearts by the Holy Spirit given to us. This was linked with the whole idea of objective revelation of God's nature and character and was very much 'given'. Without this, the content of love was hard to arrive at. 'Considering the good of others' sounded all right but had subtly smuggled in the idea of 'good' from somewhere else.

Again a useful insight, based upon a true facet of human nature. But not the *only* facet.

7. *Man is dead*

(Have no point – will despair) It is paradoxical to call this a starting-point. It is rather a reason for not starting. Yet quite a lot has been written which bears this stamp. It has links with the 'machine' viewpoint since it sees man as caught in a web of machine-like forces against which he has no power to determine anything for himself. The product of mindless evolutionary forces, doomed to extinction, he finds no purpose in life. Any claim to meaning, hope or purpose is debunked as wishful thinking, whistling in the dark. Sometimes life is made bearable with an 'eat, drink and be merry, for tomorrow we die' attitude. But after the hangover, the midnight reveller mocks himself for his folly. Sometimes nihilism is combined with a policy of political action. Burn it all down, and occasionally smuggle in the (illicit) hope that what comes from the ashes may be better. This viewpoint does not often surface at the would-be teacher level. Usually it hits folk in their student days or later when they find that the literature of despair speaks to their own lost condition. It is not usually from such ranks that teachers are recruited, and primary and secondary school syllabuses are more hopeful documents. If mid-century literature comes in the A level syllabus you are hardly expected to go along with it, but to criticize and (the syllabus writers hope) reject it.

It may sound odd to say this approach still has something true in it. Ecclesiastes is the biblical statement of 'vanity and vexation of spirit' (Ec. 2:17). True, the writer does flavour it with knowledge of a creator (to be remembered while still you are young) and 'the whole duty of man' (Ec. 12:14), but most of the time he is lamenting the emptiness and futility of life. God has set eternity in man's heart. A routine of pleasure, activity – even useful activity – and enquiry will not satisfy. Augustine again: 'We are made for Thee and our hearts find no rest until we find it in Thee.' Definitely not the only place to stand, but (as readers of Francis Schaeffer will know) sometimes a useful place to start talking to someone who knows the reality of despair and lostness in secular western society.

Still there's more to follow

What can a Christian make of all these different viewpoints? All say something true about mankind, yet none providing a framework big enough to cover all the ways in which we learn and know. There is much in all of them we can agree with, but none which we feel covers everything. Once again, Christians find themselves sounding arrogant or patronizing. Not bad, intuitionist – take a B+ ; rationalist B+ too; existentialist, a good try but only B– . Sorry if it sounds like that, and very sorry if we set out to make it sound like that. But the truth is that Christianity claims to start further back. I can fit the atheist scientist's refusal of God into my view of the world – it's already done for me in Romans chapter 1. He, or the climate of western thought, regards God as an irrelevance; he suppresses the truth. The scientist, incidentally, for his part must also explain (on his presuppositions) why I go back beyond his scientific standing-ground to God the creator. This usually involves him in an exercise in reductionism by which he shows that my belief is 'really only' the result of genetic, biochemical or environmental factors.

We all see much the same data. Christians regard this data as truly *data*, God's common *giving* to everyone. We read it how we like. Our presuppositions are the spectacles with which we read. Calvin wrote that special revelation provides the spectacles with which we read God's general revelation:

> 'For as the aged, or those whose sight is defective, when any book however fair is set before them, though they perceive that there is something written, are scarcely able to make out two consecutive words, but, when aided by glasses, begin to read distinctly, so Scripture, gathering together the impressions of Deity, which, till then, lay confused in their minds, dissipates the darkness, and shows us the true God clearly.'[13]

As we talk about life and experience with people of differing conviction, we find much to share. Humanist and Christian find themselves at least co-belligerents against unreason and prejudice, though hardly full allies. We must beware of a false Christian take-over bid which despises all other starting-points, saying everything is revealed in the Bible. Special revelation does not relieve us of the obligation to read God's other books of nature and history. The reactions of church leaders to Copernicus and Galileo (and perhaps Darwin) are instances of this mistake.

The relationship between special and general revelation is hard to define. Calvin's 'spectacles' help. Man is created *capax dei*, able to respond to God; experience can be interpreted as receiving and responding to God. So 'levels of understanding' provide a possible analogy. At one level (without 'spectacles') C. S. Lewis's *The Lion, the Witch and the Wardrobe*[14] is a pleasant children's story. At another (with the 'specs') it is a powerful story of the struggle between good and evil. Perhaps spectacles are not the happiest idea. They are useful for turning blurr into clarity, but the extra meaning does not come from reading small print. The extra comes from seeing the whole thing from a new viewpoint. Colour is in some ways a better analogy. The TV film gains impact and meaning when seen in colour; some of the dialogue becomes more fully intelligible. The characters live in a world of colour. Black-and-white viewers will miss some of the cues. If you think of black-and-white as the secular world view, then colour is nearer the biblical view. Secular humanists regard aspects of experience that survive in their black-and-white world (things like number, motion, kinematics, social interaction) as objective, 'facts' for everyone. Values, beauty, judgments, reference to God and eternity they regard as subjective, likely to differ between different people – and some possibly mistaken anyway.

The extra is not a few extra bits added to a row of experiences. 'God' is not an object among objects; he is, as Karl Barth so forcibly taught, not 'it' to be discussed, but 'He' who encounters us. The language of personal encounter again presupposes a particular viewpoint. You react differently to the waxwork 'attendant' in Madame Tussaud's from the way you react to a live one. You may make an embarrassing mistake. If the 'waxwork' you are so carefully examining suddenly twitches or winks you hastily revise your presupposition.

There is another twist to the screw, however. There is something about the live specimen which the waxwork does not have. That 'something' *demands* that you treat it differently. If you don't, then you act inappropriately, making a mistaken reduction of the living to the dead. Similarly, to discuss Christian experience, joy, praise, forgiveness, thankfulness as if they were 'only' human expressions, is to come down a step. What you are dealing with is not only 'person' but 'Christian person'. To dismiss Jesus as 'only' a figure of history, is to make a similarly false limitation. Paul makes the point clearly in 2 Corinthians 5:16ff.

How do we get this 'colour vision' that brings the full beauty and meaning? How do we get the spectacles that bring the blurr into focus? Much of the New Testament is about this very thing. Romans 10:9,17, for instance: 'If you confess "Jesus is Lord" and believe in your heart that God has raised him from the dead, you will be saved (=made whole)... faith comes by hearing, and hearing by the word of God.' This is the Christian stance, the Christian presupposition. God reveals himself; Jesus is risen Lord. There is no discontinuity between black-and-white experience and the full colour experience. Things that were true in black-and-white remain so in colour – perhaps more so. Owning Jesus as Lord will not make time go more, or less, quickly – it simply makes it *his* time that you're using; it won't make genetics or agriculture any different – it simply makes it *his* world that you're finding out about and using. The 'reality' you discover is not cut off from the world everyone else knows, but meshes with it everywhere. It is unlike the case of an LSD tripper who claims to find a totally different environment from which he has later to descend to normal life. The Hindu or Buddhist 'enlightenment' reduces the ordinary (black-and-white) experience to '*maya*', unreality or illusion, making a discontinuity between 'ordinary' and 'spiritual' experience. The Hebrew Christian doctrine of creation has no such gulf. All the 'ordinary' categories are God's creation and God keeps them going. They are part of his Word. Nature is one of his books. History is another. The lives of great believers are another (what Malcolm Muggeridge calls the 'third testament'). At any point you can put on the specs, or turn on the light and see the full meaning.

So the last twist of the screw is the hardest. This fuller knowledge is a *moral* matter. A major reason why many people do not see the full meaning is that they are unwilling to take the specs. They do not believe it to be true because they are unwilling that it should all be true. There is a reluctance to abandon some less demanding, 'lower-down' position. C. E. M. Joad's experience is an example:

'... the rationalist-optimist philosophy by the light of which I had hitherto done my best to live, came to seem intolerably trivial and superficial – a shallow-rooted plant which, growing to maturity amid the lush and leisured optimism of the nineteenth century, was quite unfitted to withstand the bleaker winds that blow through ours. I abandoned it, and in abandoning it found myself a Christian.'[15]

C. S. Lewis gives an account of how he, too, was 'brought in, kicking, struggling, resentful ... and darting his eyes in every direction for a chance of escape.'[16]

The gospels are full of people who failed to meet the real Jesus, though he was present with them. They could not break out of a self-centred or nationally-orientated life. They were even prepared to rationalize their unbelief – 'Give God the praise, we know that this man is a sinner' (Jn. 9:24). Modern Western European society shows the same sad refusal to accept the whole meaning. One of the cleverest, most affluent and technologically equipped eras of human history is marked by a lack of dimension that makes it an age of despair.

The Spens Report said that children should be made aware of the possibility of a religious interpretation of life. Tell them where they can find the spectacles. That is quite as much a necessary part of education today as it was in 1938.

1 *Spectrum*, Vol. 10 no. 2, 1978.
2 D. M. MacKay, *The clockwork image* (IVP, 1974).
3 D. Morris, *The Naked Ape* (Cape, 1967).
4 J. Lewis and B. Towers, *Naked Ape or Homo Sapiens?* (The Garstone Press, 1969).

5 J. H. Jacques, *The Right and the Wrong* (SPCK, 1965).
6 C. S. Lewis, *The Abolition of Man* (Geoffrey Bles, 1946).
7 M. Ginsberg, *On the Diversity of Morals* (Heinemann, 1956).
8 J. Wilson, N. Williams and B. Sugarman, *Introduction to Moral Education* (Penguin, 1967).
9 R. S. Peters and P. H. Hirst, *The Logic of Education* (Routledge & Kegan Paul, 1970).
10 P. H. Hirst, *Moral Education in a Secular Society* (University of London Press & National Children's Home, 1974).
11 J. A. T. Robinson, *Honest to God* (SCM Press, 1963).
12 J. Fletcher, *Situation Ethics* (SCM Press, 1966).
13 J. Calvin, *Institutes*, I. VI.
14 C. S. Lewis, *The Lion, the Witch and the Wardrobe* (Puffin, 1959)
15 C. E. M. Joad, *Recovery of Belief* (Faber, 1962).
16 C. S. Lewis, *Surprised by Joy* (Fontana, 1959).

5. How to live with the sociology of education

Sociology of some sort or another features in the professional training of many people – probation officers, social workers, personnel managers, town and country planners, even doctors, all get a dose of sociology here and there. So you are not alone in undergoing this particular trial of your faith (or educational opportunity), and may be moved to ask 'What is it about sociology that gets it a place in so many courses?'. If you can understand why you're doing sociology it might be easier to resolve any particularly 'Christian' difficulties over the subject. Not that there need be any difficulties but for many Christian students, going to sociology lectures seems to be regarded in the same light as accepting lifts from strangers. What is sociology? What is it trying to tell you? What is it trying to do?

At least one student thought the aim of sociology was to make you a socialist; another, perhaps more naïvely, thought it was to make you sociable. Both wrong; try again. The bits of paper they give you at the beginning of term tell you that one of the aims of the course is to look at education 'with a sociological perspective'. Books are apt to say that sociology isn't a collection of facts but 'a way of looking at things'. So here is a course which actually sets out to do something to you: to change the way you look at things and think about them. It's not just asking you to memorize a lot of facts and trot them out at examination time, but to think about other facts from an approach that you may not have considered before. You could of course ignore the urge to 'think sociologically', to 'get a sociological perspective'. You could just amass yet another folder full of notes and hope to get by with judicious quotation and regurgitation in the examination. But it may not work; it won't be very satisfactory; and anyway Christians of all people should be prepared to explore and test, listen and judge, rather than clam up or opt out.

Does it matter?

It is not only Christian students who let slip the occasional critical comment about sociology. Many of your fellow students will be groaning too. Why have they got to bother us with it? We shall teach our children geography, history, mathematics or whatever just as well without it. Isn't it just complicated common sense or, at worst, finding ingenious excuses for naughty children? Most of the groans are second-hand, of course, because the groaners haven't actually experienced the treatment.

Does it matter? Some of your friends may even be unconvinced about the need to have any perspective at all. You may feel great one-upmanship because you have a 'Christian' perspective, so why add a sociological one? Of course your Christian faith should influence everything seven days a week but that doesn't stop you taking advantage of anything else that helps fill out the picture. As a mature (or, perhaps more modestly, maturing) Christian you can supplement, support, modify and enrich your faith, learn new things from new experiences (and teaching is certainly a new experience!). No need to be defensive about it, but actively look for opportunities of interacting with other viewpoints – in this case, sociology.

Before looking at the reasons sociologists give for thinking their stall worth patronizing, there are two other niggling ideas you might find lurking in your mind. First, neutrality is a mirage. If you pretend to be uninterested in sociology, you are in fact taking a negative stance towards it. It's like the folk who think themselves broadminded because they don't let their kids do RE, or hear about Christian faith 'till they're old enough to judge it for themselves'. They forget that they've given the children the biggest possible lesson, that Christianity isn't worth worrying about yet. So, in regarding sociology as a chore to be endured, you are not being splendidly neutral (even if you don't join the groaners), but proclaiming that this area of study is not worth attention. You need strong reasons for saying that. And further, you won't end up with 'no sociology', but with a mish-mash of ideas that you've picked up unconsciously here and there. So when staff-room conversation turns to streaming, or the influence of the media, or unemployment, you'll contribute (as most of your colleagues will, regrettably,) and talk off the top of your head a bit of common sense garnished with whatever prejudices you've accumulated in whatever sort of educational process you've undergone.

The second niggle concerns the origins of sociology. It started in a self-consciously secular way. Comte, Spencer, Marx were carried along on the wave of apparent success of science (even Science with a capital 'S') in a climate of thought that was progressively unsympathetic to biblical faith. They set out not only to give an alternative to Christianity but even to account for the rise of Christianity in terms of their own analyses and presuppositions. Maybe it's a pity it started that way, but that's how it was – a secular, independent understanding of community. A pity, too, because it need not have been that way. If Christian people had been in at the start, joining in the debate, things might have been different. But they weren't, and by the time the great sociological industry got going forty or fifty years ago, the 'alternative' image was firmly fixed, and not surprisingly a lot of people regard it not only as 'alternative' but as 'opposition'. Now that Christians are beginning to get in

57

on the debate, a more fruitful dialogue is possible. But it's another example of Moody's dictum that 'A lie gets half way round the world before truth gets its boots on' – not that sociology is necessarily a lie; just one part of truth which might be lop-sided on its own.

The reasons usually put forward for including sociology of education in a college course include:

1. It does in fact contribute indirectly to classroom practice, in that it enables teachers to 'put their jobs into a wider social perspective and thus be better prepared to understand the difficulties of pupils in certain types of areas'.[1]

2. Put rather more positively, and perhaps more controversially, it allows teachers to take on the task of 'cultural missionary'.

3. It contributes to the general education of the student by providing the sort of things 'educated persons should know'. P. Berger says that to ask a sociological question 'presupposes that one is interested in looking some distance beyond the commonly accepted or officially defined goals of human action. It presupposes a certain awareness that human events have different levels of meaning, some of which are hidden from the consciousness of everyday life. It may even presuppose a measure of suspicion about the way in which human events are officially interpreted by the authorities, be they political, juridical or religious in character.'[2]

4. Thus it not only provides the student with things educated people should know but presents them in such a way as to increase awareness of oneself and one's place in the educational system in particular and society in general.

Whether what actually goes on in sociology departments supports this is another matter. But even if you want to sue them under the trades description acts, you must agree that there are some useful goods to sell. Not specifically Christian, of course, but insights that could help you understand a bit better yourself and others in God's world. Whether there are specifically Christian items that could go on the sociology stall is something to look at in a page or two, but for the moment let us take a quick tour round the 'black-and-white' sociology scene, see what secular sociologists are doing. Then we can decide whether there's anything we want to add, or see in 'colour'.

What sort of people do they think we are?

Scientists

For some time, sociology was seen as a science. At some stage you will almost certainly come across Musgrave's *The Sociology of Education*[3] in which he says:

> 'Sociology is a social science ... A science should contain no prejudice. Therefore a sociology of education must give neutral analysis. Politics must be avoided ... on the whole we shall be concerned with means and not ends, but *sometimes* we shall be brought to the point *beyond which a sociologist can no longer go* without taking up a philosophical position'. (italics added)

and in the conclusion of the same book:

> 'The aims of education have not been central to the argument. The sociology of education considers how the educational system works with given aims. This book has on the whole dealt with problems of means, not ends, though this is no reason for the teacher to study the sociology of education and to ignore its philosophy.'

This point of view separates sociology very sharply from philosophy. It is definitely in the science category, where (it is claimed) all talk of metaphysics, politics, religion and value is out of place. This point of view is hotly disputed at the present time, but it is likely you will meet it either from older textbooks, or lecturers who have not updated their notes from the lecturers they listened to years ago. So it is worth looking at the presuppositions underlying it.

The scientific approach itself makes a number of presuppositions — for example, that there is a real universe to look at; that the universe is regular (what happens today will happen in similar circumstances tomorrow); that cause-and-effect is the key to understanding what goes on. These presuppositions do not appear to involve the observer. That is, the universe is regular for whoever looks at it: whether you are Christian, Buddhist, atheist or Zoroastrian, $g = 9.81$ ms^{-2} and provided you do the right experiments, you can prove it. The main outcome of all this is said to be that science is value-free or 'neutral as regards values'. You may not like to think of thousands of Jews dying in gas-chambers; Hitler may have revelled in it; but from the scientific viewpoint, as the chemist Haber researched it, gas at that concentration simply *does* kill whether you like it or not. Which introduces the sting in the scientific tail. Your liking or disliking does not alter the fact. In the scientific account everything is 'caused', and the whole of experience is knit together in a web of necessity. 'Che sera, sera, whatever will be will be' is the theme song of the scientific method.

So, if sociology is a science, it will give you an explanation of community in terms of cause-and-effect, how each part of the system functions to keep the whole show going. It will deal in wide generalizations (as science can't tell you what any particular electron will do, but can say with confidence what a few millions will do), so that you won't know precisely which housewife will change from 'Fizz' to 'Fazz' because of the advert, but on average 20,000 will. In just the same way as the scientist was seen as a detached person, observing from outside what was happening in his test-tubes, so the sociologist was a detached observer, watching how each part of society fulfilled its function in keeping the whole system going. In practice he had a slightly tougher time than the scientist because it was harder to do the experiments. You can test metals to destruction to find out more about them, but no-one will let you do the experiment of shooting students who fail examinations to see if it improves performance of those who survive. Even in natural science there is a whole range of possible 'causes' to investigate. In sociology the matter is even more complicated and one of the criticisms rightly levelled at some sociological research is that the researcher is too easily satisfied that he has found *the* cause of this or that behaviour.

Thirty years ago science enjoyed an aura of great authority and finality, 'value-free', 'objective', not tied to any religious or philosophical system. Sociology tended to jump on the same bandwagon. Nowadays science is seen as *one* (very useful) explanation of experience, a useful tool with which we go to work on experience, but a tool that must be used, intelligently, with willed and responsible decision. Sociology is also moving in the same direction.

Scientists who care

The move in sociology is partly because of the sort of people who are involved. Very often they are *not* detached observers, but are where the action is. They care passionately about the conditions they investigate; they want to *improve* conditions for the people they meet. So they smuggle in (or sometimes boldly declare at the ideological customs barrier) presuppositions of their own. At the very least they have, for example,

> 'the assertion that man is fundamentally rational (or irrational) or that society is inherently stable (or unstable)... in other words a presupposition about the nature of things which is ultimately determined by one's religious viewpoint. Assertions of this kind are unverifiable and must be accepted by some sort of intuitive faith. One may say, with Marx, that man's 'natural' state is 'species-being' (that is, unconstrained, purposive activity in work) but this is not observable in

the empirical sense. It is an article of faith, a presupposition'.[4]

Other presuppositions will soon be unearthed with a little care. Some may concern the interaction of people and events. People can interpret symbols in various ways; they can respond to different codes of language; they can adopt differing roles and place other people in a variety of roles; and all of these are open not only to manipulation by those on the outside but to change from the actors on the inside. So the 'necessity' image of the scientific view slips a little. People are no longer reduced to being cogs in a machine, but allowed at least the 'freedom' of actors in a play, experiencing emotions and frustrations. In some versions they may even *ad-lib* a little and alter a scene or two.

Further along the line you will come to sociologists who care deeply about the people and communities they study. They are against poverty, exploitation, despair, so their writings tend not only to describe inner city life but to condemn it.

One sociologist recently called sociological theories 'doctrines' to emphasize his belief that they are combinations of judgments of value as well as of fact. They contain social philosophies as well as systems of concepts and propositions. Another sociologist suggests that sociological theories define and explain behaviour from 'socially situated value positions'.

Here-and-now men

This is the polite, positive term for 'rootless men' or 'men with no absolutes'. To keep the positive emphasis for a while, this approach is good in that it concentrates attention on the actual area of research. If you want to find out how the Bashem Islands maintain law and order you must go and look, try to understand how they see their customs and structures, and not judge it by the standards of city businessmen or a few Celtic fans. Your first question is 'What is it like to be a Bashem Islander;

how would I think and feel if I'd been brought up here instead of in Wigan?'. All very good, and it might have helped if early 'civilizers' and missionaries had used a touch of this approach in dealing with tribal dancing, hunting rituals and even marriage customs.

But now for the bad news. This here-and-now emphasis can become 'cultural relativism'. This suggests that everything is relative to the time, place and culture in which it happens. Nothing wrong so far, perhaps, but the theory then goes on to argue (in splendid pseudo-logic, because it doesn't follow at all) that you must not judge them by 'our' standards. In this sort of sociological foray (not to call it a debate) you may be pointing out how the breakdown of family life is putting intolerable strains on schoolchildren, only to be told that the concept of 'family life' is a recent western invention and that in many places all sorts of loose liaisons and uncontrolled sexual goings-on abound and children still grow up. At a more down-to-earth level, you may be told that whatever life-style you practised at 76 Yew Tree Gardens in Suburbia, you've no right to criticize what goes on in K Block of Bloggs College. So a new presupposition is smuggled in; there are no absolutes, no principles of relationship or morality that apply everywhere. This is odd, because such people readily agree that scientific laws apply everywhere – poison kills in the Bashem Islands and selfishness leads to rivalry which leads to violence. Yet it is not agreed that selfishness is wrong and that social structures should aim to control it.

A recent variant on the cultural relativity theme is the notion of the relativity of knowledge. Knowledge has expanded so rapidly, it is said, that we are in a distinctly different situation from all generations before us. Therefore statements of value that might have been valid when people knew much less are no longer valid. Certainly the expansion of knowledge opens up possibilities that were not there before. Different modes of production offer the possibility of a more complex (and perhaps more satisfying?) style of life, and certainly more leisure time. Increased communications offer the possibility of much wider interaction between more groups of people. Safe contraception offers marital (and extra-marital) relationships very different from those of the past.

All this is true, and the explosion of knowledge faces Christian and unbeliever alike with challenges. The new understanding of the world and its possibilities is no less God-given (in the Christian view) than the original world, so we have more raw material to work with than our forefathers. The mistake comes when it is said that 'therefore' (another bit of pseudo-logic) all the moral and religious thinking of the centuries must be scrapped because women take pills and men go to the moon. Even if babies are grown in test tubes instead of the traditional methods used hitherto, their worth, status and responsibility as individuals will still need to be determined. And the thinking done when babies were born by steam-age methods will still have a lot to contribute. Even if alternative sources of energy are discovered, the debate about the use of the world's resources (and particularly its distribution among the haves and the have-nots) will be very relevant. It is too easy to import presuppositions which deny absolutes, (principles of value which apply to everyone, everywhere, always). It is also deceptively easy to camouflage them so that they do not look like the presuppositions they are. They are sometimes dressed up to look like 'results of investigation'.

One disastrous by-product of the relativistic view of culture and knowledge is that society has no compass. The teeth are drawn from every attempt to criticize structures or practice. Whereas traditionally prophets and thinkers have criticized their societies, usually by reference to established principles of value and duty, now the wisdom of the past is not only past but *passé*, out-of-date, not relevant today. Knowledge (like technology) becomes servant not judge of society. In educational terms, for example, if we are short of engineers a sociologist can be called in to tell us how to get more engineers. After all, the meat factory can switch from pork pies to sausage rolls to meet demands, and so a 'production' model of the school can be dealt with in the same way. Whether pupils should be so directed cannot be answered by reference to old-fashioned ideas of individuality, creativity, calling. In practice the market, or the national interest, determines what is 'right'. Today's needs are judge; knowledge built up over centuries must see they are met.

Christian people?

Are there any specifically Christian presuppositions that should be brought to the study of sociology? Are Christian sociologists really ordinary sociologists with a different jersey, or an extra pair of eyes, or another column headed 'Christian' in their notebooks? To go back to the 'black-and-white *v.* colour' analogy of a previous section, it has been argued that Christians can use the techniques and frameworks of secular sociologists but put them into a wider view of the world as a whole. In particular they are put into the wider framework of the world as *God's* world, with men and women, not as detached observers, but 'workers together with God' (2 Cor. 6:1). So, to the concept of understanding and control (of the secular sociologist) are added the concepts of wonder, thankfulness and obedience. The scientist becomes the worshipping, thankful, responsible scientist. The scientist who cares becomes the scientist who cares in God's name. The here-and-now man attempts to relate the eternal purpose and power to the opportunities of the here-and-now. On this view, sociology becomes one of the tools God has given to mankind with which to service the world. It comes as part of a package for being human that includes many other things – like absolutes, ideas of human dignity and accountability, ideals of love, obedience, reconciliation, worship. The package includes the presuppositions of natural science, a real, intelligible, reliable world in which cause-and-effect is a useful interpretative tool. It excludes such presuppositions as cultural relativity and ethical neutrality.

All too often Christian people have reacted as if being Christian was an optional extra they happen to have signed up for. They have been content (so the caricature goes) to compartmentalize their lives, keeping work to weekdays and worship for Sundays. Sociology could survive on weekdays, being taken out of its cupboard only after the Christian perspectives of Sunday had been reverently put away after evening prayer. This is probably overdrawn, but over and over again students present the 'compartment' symptoms. Bible study and prayer rarely interact for them with physics, literature or education. They even seem unaware that there ought to be or could be any such interaction, except perhaps at the level of personal behaviour. They would not cheat in examinations or attempt to seduce the lecturer, but they do not see it as part of their Christian commitment to criticize the examination syllabus or the lecturer's presuppositions.

In sharp reaction against this has been a school of thought which sees anything Christian as so distinctively different from anything secular that it requires a fresh start, from specifically Christian presuppositions. According to this view the whole of Western European thought structures are hopelessly enmeshed in humanistic presuppositions and a world-view, and nothing less than wholesale criticism by Christian standards will do. Christians are called to proclaim and live by the absolute sovereignty of God over every aspect of life, and to serve God with heart, mind and strength in every realm of life. In such service, any compromise with the humanist-secularist systems of present society could be ruinous, and (at one extreme) this view can be used to justify Christian withdrawal from present schools and universities and the founding of specifically Christian institutions. The position is cogently argued in, *e.g.*, H. Dooyeweerd, *A New*

Critique of Theoretical Thought.[5] A brief statement of the position, and a criticism of it, is given as far as sociology is concerned in *Christian Commitment and the Study of Sociology*.[6]

Back to school

It may be helpful to relate what has been said so far to an educational context. This is, after all, where you are most likely to meet sociological questions, and particular features of schools and schoolchildren will highlight the principles involved.

You may already have come across books written from a Christian viewpoint that deal with education. Perhaps it was these that made you think of education as a worthwhile field of work; though you may not have analysed what you read to pick out the 'Christian' bits, if in fact there are any. But such writing gives a place to start thinking:

'Education should fit a young person to take his place as a member of adult society ... will encourage the fullest expression of the possibilities for good in each child, whether physical, intellectual, emotional or spiritual.'[7]

'Education will help to develop God-given natural gifts, whether academic, practical or personal. It will teach techniques for controlling the material world and developing the external resources that God has given to mankind for his use. It will help people to understand the world as it really is and thereby lead to a great respect for the law of God. No teacher can fail to inculcate some attitude to justice, truth and help for the underprivileged. The very fact of studying God's creation faces us with structures that He has imparted and should develop a respect for the created order and its Creator and a sense of certain basic moral duties.'[8]

'Education is the nurture of personal growth ... concerned not only (or even chiefly) with the communication of knowledge and the acquisition of skill, but also with the formation of right attitudes – attitudes towards learning, towards work, towards truth and goodness, towards other people, towards life in general. Education, moreover, is a person-to-person activity; it can function only when there is personal communication under conditions of mutual respect.'[9]

These quotations are clearly concerned with aims, values, ideals. The 'is' in 'education is' represents an ideal to aim at, not a detached description of a process. They are, if you like, strategic plans rather than tactical reports; they say what ought to happen, rather than how to do it or the scene in which it must be done.

By comparison, the work you will do in sociology of education will seem very remote from ideals and long-term plans. But in fact, some of the interests of the sociology of education have found some of their roots in Christian concern (such as equality and justice) in a way that much of the general sociological scene has not. For example, one of the primary interests of the sociology of education has been to establish and explain the differential performance of working class as compared to middle class children in educational institutions. This developed out of studies of social stratification and the division of labour in society. It arose from a belief that the study of educational institutions was the key to understanding the process of social stratification. Virtually all British sociologists of education have been at least implicitly concerned with social class inequalities in schooling, and the 'wastage of talent' arising from unequal access to a highly selective educational system. Halsey, for example, looked at the pre-school environment as the real root of inequality; others looked within the school and argued that streaming was a main cause of underachievement. These were essentially investigations of what was happening, matters of concern to educators which the sociologists took up as subjects for their research.

The relation between theory and action has already been hinted at in the quotation from Musgrave (p. 59). He spoke of the 'point beyond which the sociologist can no longer go'. Others suggest that a person must take off his sociologist's cap and don his citizen's cap and act upon his theories. There is less support nowadays for this distinction between the *study* of behaviour and society, and our inevitable *involvement*, because we are human, with behaviour and society. Marxists use the term 'praxis' to refer to 'post-theoretical action', a synthesis of being and thought or facts and acts. This idea of merging theory and practice has a central place in Marxist thought. But why should Marxists have all the best praxis? Christians of all people ought to know about mixing belief and action, faith and works, working out their faith in daily life. Certainly many in the sociology of education business have tried to go beyond the mere publishing of research findings. The picture of sociology as a discipline in which no one is prepared to commit themselves is not true of the educational variety. Of course such involvement poses problems; research findings are one thing, how you assess them is another and what you do about them is yet another. The assessment may be a matter of professional expertise, comparing results with what has been found before, trying to account for differences. How you use them calls into play the whole scale of values and political or religious ideologies. Some early sociologists of education will be remembered by their political reports rather than as theoretical sociologists (*e.g.*, Halsey and Newsom).

One element of 'praxis' that has been the subject of sociological study is the part played by the teacher as *participant* in the classroom, the place above all others where he is certainly involved! Most studies on the role of the teacher in the classroom have been based on the sociological tradition which uses a 'consensus' model of society. In this model society is seen as

> 'a relatively stable, persistent and well integrated structure of elements ... every element in a society has a function which contributes to the system's maintenance or equilibrium of survival; and every functioning social structure is based on a consensus of values among its members.' (Colquhoun)

The teacher's function in this model is to socialize pupils into the norms and values of the social system, so that they will fulfil *their* roles to keep the show on the road. To many people this seems an excellent idea, making for stability, introducing children into the national heritage, passing on the wisdom of the past, and so on. There are some question-marks however that Christians would need to put – and which have been put increasingly by sociologists of many beliefs in recent years – on this stable, self-perpetuating model of society. Do we want to induct children into society as it is now? (Romans 12 suggests a definite 'no' to some parts of it.) Does this view respect the child's potential and individuality? Or does it treat children as passive, receptive, absorptive, rather than active, creative, inquisitive? Is it right to start with the system and look at how people are fitted into it?

So there have been a lot of new directions, starting from different views of what man is. Man is a 'creator of meaning' a 'world producer' not a 'social product'. At first glance these appear a bit more hopeful, but as they develop they seem to run into some of the difficulties mentioned earlier about cultural relativism. If you start from society, you seem to end up denying the significance of the individual child. If you start from the child as initiator it is difficult to put any yardstick beside him and so you end up in a relativistic mess. It begins to look as if we need 'something bigger than both of us', and Peter Berger (a sociologist warmly sympathetic to the Christian viewpoint) contributed some useful ideas in a book that may well turn up on a reading list – *A Rumour of Angels*.[10] Its subtitle – 'Modern society and the rediscovery of the supernatural' – gives the general idea of the book.

'The relativisers are relativised; the debunkers are debunked ... What follows is *not*, as some of the early sociologists of knowledge feared, a total paralysis of thought. Rather it is a new freedom and flexibility in asking questions of truth.'

The urge to show how everything depends upon its setting, to see through everything, has not produced the bare, certain facts. Indeed, as C. S. Lewis said long ago, it quite obviously could not. It might be nice to see through the front of the house to discover what folk inside are doing, but if you also see through them, and the back wall of the house and the hedge behind, you end up 'seeing' nothing at all. The more you succeed in seeing through things, the less point there is in sight. So in sociology you can go on saying that this, that or the other culture or structure produces this, that or the other system of values or relationships. But sooner or later you have to decide between all these values and relationships and ask which are right and which are mistaken. Is there some way of judging such things? This is a little removed from the strict interests of sociology, but is territory where Christians should recognize a landmark or two and feel they have something to contribute. Questions on the nature of man, the nature of society, the purpose of life are 'further back' than questions of how mixed ability grouping affects the way children learn arithmetic, or how corporal punishment modifies behaviour in different classes of children. But all the various research findings will sooner or later leave you with a lot of questions about the rights and wrongs of what goes on in school. The facts unearthed by research may be unpalatable, may not fit with established prejudice, may call into question accepted interpretations even of biblical passages. So folk with sociological training are sometimes viewed with suspicion in church circles; they seem always to know inconvenient facts; there is, as one writer put it, something inevitably subversive about sociology. Berger himself sees sociology as a 'debunking discipline', exposing the inadequate idols people make of social institutions and customs. He describes the tension he finds in being a Christian sociologist – in research and analysis he is a 'methodological atheist' but the facts must be set alongside a Christian interpretation. Similarly his Christian practice must be open to analysis and all the sociological questions he can ask.

Surviving sociology

So if you're embarked upon a sociology of education course the general message is 'Make the best of it.' Don't expect it to provide all the answers; on the other hand don't expect it to be totally misleading. Use it to arouse your own enquiry. It is not an infallible science but, on its own presuppositions, it does offer a tool-kit for finding out some of the ways in which society works. To change the metaphor, it provides you with a diving board from which to dive into a critical exploration of the world of education. The higher the diving board, the deeper you can plunge and not just skim about on the surface. With your Christian understanding and confidence you should have no fears about what you might find. In fact your understanding of human sinfulness should make you unshockable, and your understanding of man's redeemability should make you a final optimist. The fact that you may meet a number of unbelievers swimming at various depths need not perplex you. God in his 'common' or 'sustaining' grace has made the world so that anyone who takes the trouble can learn a lot about it. You might even find it a good point from which to start suggesting to other swimmers that people and society are not without company in the universe.

1 J. H. Newsom, *Half our future* (HMSO, 1963).
2 P. L. Berger, *Invitation to sociology* (Penguin, 1966).

3 P. W. Musgrave, *The Sociology of Education* (Methuen, 1972).
4 D. Lyon, *Christians and sociology* (IVP, 1975).
5 H. Dooyeweerd, *A New Critique of Theoretical Thought* (available from the Christian Studies Unit).
6 ed. A. Walter, *Christian commitment and the study of sociology* (available from UCCF Bookstall, Nottingham).
7 P. Cousins, *Education and Christian Parents* (Scripture Union, 1969).
8 A. N. Triton, *Whose world?* (IVP, 1970).
9 M. V. C. Jeffreys, *Personal Values in the Modern World* (Penguin, 1962).
10 P. L. Berger, *A Rumour of Angels* (Penguin, 1971).

6. Psychology for psaints?

As with sociology, so with psychology. It seems to have had a poor press in some Christian circles – one of the 'things to be careful about', like drinking water abroad. Among education students in general it has a poor press, being regarded as boring (like most other lectures), a waste of time, a way of finding complicated reasons for common sense, another excuse for tedious essays. You almost get a sneaking admiration for the psychology lecturers who press on in the face of the opposition, inertia or ill-will of many of their customers. Do they deserve it? What is it about psychology that raises the temperature?

Some students get a dull 'you-can't-win' feeling. Whatever you say can be explained away with some super-psychological answer. If you're religious, then Freud said you're adapting to frustration, projecting the attributes of an earthly father onto God. If you retort that Freud naturally thought like that since he didn't like *his* father and hated his Roman Catholic nanny, you make the score 15 all. But the expert knows a lot more shots than you do so you'll lose the game and set and may as well 'go quiet', make a few notes, dash off another essay and go to the CU meeting. Only the hardiest extraverts keep up a long campaign to 'put the lecturer straight'.

Some less aggressive souls sit quietly and apprehensively in ever-increasing insecurity. All their fancied opinions and beliefs seem threatened with exposure as simply the result of social learning, psychological inevitabilities of their class and upbringing.

The very words seem weighted against you. Your approach to experience is anecdotal, unsystematic, naïve and probably prejudiced, certainly not objective, systematized by reference to standardized norms and such like respectable practices. You could reply with a 'horses for courses' argument – for example, systematized courtship by reference to standardized norms is not as much fun as the anecdotal, naïve sort – but still you feel a bit out of your depth in the sophisticated atmosphere where everything is so well explained and buttoned up.

Beat them or join them?

Perhaps it wasn't a good idea to start this chapter this way. You may have begun hoping it would give you irresistible ammunition for use in the war against godless psychologists. You now fear a grovelling 'but ...'. Actually, you're quite right (apart from the grovel). You are about to be invited to drop all battle and conflict metaphors, to stop feeling threatened by, or hostile towards, psychology and prepare for a cool steady look at what psychology is, and how it relates to a Christian view of children and their education.

Your textbooks will tell you that psychology is the scientific study of animal and human behaviour. There's no reason to quibble about that just because it's in a psychology textbook. 'Study' means you won't get the answer by coffee-drinking and general chat. There is evidence to look at, order to find, a lot of work already done to help you in your search. 'Scientific' means that the study will be conducted according to the presuppositions of science (as outlined previously) – a real world, a regular world, cause-and-effect relations that can be discovered by accurate observation and test. It will also draw on more mathematics than you may wish, with the statistical jargon of means, standard deviations, significance testing and so on. It is a 'scientific study'. *One* way of looking at animal and human behaviour. It is not the same as a novelist's attempt to interpret the emotional experiences of a murderer on the run, or a rabbit on Watership Down. Nor need it be in competition with the novelist's account. It is not the same as a theological king (who happened also to be an adulterous murderer) writing Psalm 32 or Psalm 51 about his experience of guilt before God. It is probable that adulterous, murdering kings who have had a strong religious background will experience feelings of guilt and express these in theological terms. A scientific study could be conducted of such people. It could describe 'how' events influenced their behaviour, words and feelings. It could never say whether or not David's sense of sin and subsequent forgiveness was true or real. Once again we have accounts that can be complementary, not competitive.

So you are embarking upon a scientific study and if your textbooks seem to leave God out it may be that they are faithfully doing their job of sticking to scientific presuppositions and methods and telling you what has been discovered and how it fits together so far. In fact, you might spare a little suspicion for the scientist who gives you five chapters of sound science and a last chapter of philosophy/religion/social comment. This seems to be an occupational hazard of paperback authors from Hoyle writing about the universe to B. F. Skinner writing about conditioned behaviour. The mantle of astronomer or psychologist is suddenly changed for the prophetic robe.

Beyond the evidence

In many cases the writers are quite clear what is happening. They know when they move from scientific observation and description to moral judgment and social prescription. So Eysenck says quite frankly:

> 'Facts may help us in deciding upon the means, but they do not furnish us with the ends: morality tells us about the ends, but leaves us the task of finding the

77

means. It is only when both sets of premises are kept in harmony that socially useful and valuable action can result.'[1]

You may not agree entirely with the rest of his paragraph but at least he is not claiming that his psychological expertise and authority carry over into his social commentary. Raymond Cattell concludes a monumental work on abilities (500 pages of most detailed research and analysis, together with suggestions such as artificial insemination by highly intelligent donors to 'improve' the average ability) with the words: 'Certainly intelligence is valueless, or even positively dangerous, unless it is the servant of character and clear moral values.' Not every author is so frank, and those who popularize their findings are even less clear. Malcolm Jeeves states his concern as follows:

'... as someone principally engaged in what is variously called pure research or fundamental research, I have to confess an increasing concern about how the result of such research is at times presented to teachers in training and how extrapolations, some very difficult to justify, seem so readily to be made from it. What is most disturbing is the way in which extrapolations once made so readily become established dogma. I shall give some examples of this later. There are, of course, many instances in which such over-enthusiastic and, perhaps, premature applications of the results of psychological research to the practice of education do no great harm, even if they do little good.

Having said that, I must add that I have become increasingly concerned about the over-zealous acceptance by *some*, including educationists, of tentative findings from psychological research and about the subsequent propagandist zeal with which they have been given widespread and, I shall argue, premature, application. Moreover, insufficient care has been taken to distinguish between the findings being reported and

> the personal philosophies, values and ideologies of the
> advocates concerned.'[2]

We must therefore learn to distinguish the scientific findings from the value judgments with which they may be intertwined. Jeeves concludes a short summary of the work of B. F. Skinner:

> 'To conclude this brief discussion of Skinner. First, we must carefully distinguish between the scientific contribution made by him and his colleagues, and the extrapolations that have been made from it, and uses to which such knowledge has been and may be put. Secondly, we must distinguish between the scientific contribution made by Skinner, and his own personal values. It does seem clear that, as regards his wider views, he is ethically naive and that he embraces some kind of philosophy of evolutionism linked with a reductionist view of man. He is thus a supporter of a view of man which is at best sub-Christian and at worst anti-Christian.'[3]

Distinguishing takes time and effort. The worst extrapolators are journalists, pushed for time, faced with a flow of 100-page reports upon which they have to comment for readers who are interested only in the unusual. My own favourite is the headline in the *Wolverhampton Express and Star*, 'Marx may oust pupil prayers', as a summary of the twenty essays published by NFER as *Progress and Problems in Moral Education.*[4] (It is true that in one essay John Hull did mention that a society that is already plural in its faiths should cease to try and nurture all children in a single religion but should teach children about the whole range of world-views.) However, one advantage of spending three years – at enormous public expense – in an institution of learning is that you can look at the reports themselves and learn the skills of assessing the evidence. You may have neither time nor inclination to read the whole shelf of Piaget, but there must be a compromise between reading the lot and just soaking up the potted version in the textbook – what one examiner calls 'the non-critical assimilation of pre-digested Piaget (of whom much is said but little read)'.

There is still more to be said about this distinguishing, critical business. If you dismiss all the psychology in your course as an evil to be endured as briefly and painlessly as possible, you will not be achieving monumental neutrality. You will end up, not with *no* psychology, but with whatever bits and pieces you have picked up from hearsay, native wit and occasional observation. You may not know what connectionists or field-cognition theories say about learning, but you will still have your own ideas of how the little horrors ought to learn. Even if it is only

Ram it in, jam it in, children's heads are hollow:
Slam it in, cram it in, still there's more to follow.

You will have some theory of learning which will influence your future performance as a teacher. You will probably spatter a mark-book with marks and have some idea of what you think the assessment shows. You will have some ideas about what curriculum ought to contain, what children ought to be able to learn at various stages, what is 'too difficult' and what 'anyone can do'.

It is no crime to have arrived at your present stage with this colourful rag-bag of ideas and impressions – it might even be commendable evidence that you have thought about things a bit already. But it would be blameworthy if you did not take the opportunity to test out your ideas against other people's and to look at all the evidence you can about the children you are going to teach. Evidence, note, not directives or gospel. Evidence to be weighed. Who did the work? Where? (Research done in America does not always cross the Atlantic intact.) How does it fit with other findings? Did he have an axe to grind? The examiner quoted above even dared to add: 'Student teachers, and even student teachers who are parents, have tended to ignore the evidence of their own experience in favour of the Piagetian view, such is the strength of the

Piagetian legend.' Your own experience is part of the evidence. In particular your own Christian experience is a kind of evidence that some researchers may lack, may suspect or even reduce to some other category.

You will, in fact, find that this question of evidence divides writers on psychology into two broad camps. Many, following the older workers, regard introspection as valuable evidence. It is right and useful to ask people to express their feelings, talk about their attitudes, values, hopes and fears. It is right and useful to try and watch *yourself* thinking. It all helps to understand how the mind works, the personality grows, and thought patterns confirm or change. Others (notably the behaviourists) are suspicious of taking anybody's word for anything. To them, evidence is what can actually be observed. If Jill says she wants to be a nurse because she wants to help people, all you can observe is that she said so; you might perhaps infer that she thinks so, but certainly not that it *is* so. Gilbert Ryle expressed this view of evidence:

> 'Those human actions and reactions, those spoken and unspoken utterances, those tones of voice, facial expression and gestures, which have always been the data of all other students of men, have, after all, been the right and only manifestations to study.[5]

Ryle was trying to clear up 'great verbal muddle' (and 'primarily ... trying to get some disorders out of (his) own system', p. 10) in which traits of character get smuggled in as if they were events. 'He did no homework because of his laziness' introduces 'laziness' as an efficient cause that accounts for something. Whereas in fact 'lazy' simply is a shorthand for 'He does nothing in the absence of strong stimulus such as reward or punishment.' Ryle talks about 'unpacking' statements about disposition: so 'vanity' is unpacked to give: 'Whenever situations of certain sorts have arisen, he has always or usually tried to make himself prominent.' This could lead to a form of reductionism in which 'vanity' was said to be meaningless, or just a shorthand. It is only fair to say that Ryle does not appear to intend this: he recognizes, for instance, that 'skill' can properly be attributed to a situation, 'not as something that could be separately recorded by a camera', but something logically distinct, another way of talking about the incident. The tightrope walker got across successfully, and in so doing showed his skill. But showing skill is not the same kind of behaviour as putting one foot in front of the other.

The scientific emphasis – in the sense of collecting and analysing data about observable behaviour – has an impressive literature, and has yielded a lot of statistical facts. (The argument is not usually about the facts, but about the interpretation of the facts.) Assuming that there is something constant about the human species, you can say what is likely and unlikely in the response of a group of children to particular situations.

An alternative emphasis in recent years has been dubbed 'humanist'. This does not have to be an anti-Christian word, by the way. Remember Peter's 'I also am a man.' 'Humanist' only becomes an 'anti' word when it claims there is *nothing but* human intelligence, power or resource around. The humanist school emphasizes the wholeness of personality and is less interested in masses of numerical data than in how a person experiences, recognizes, makes decisions. Hence for them introspective evidence is very important. At some stage you will probably be referred to Carl Rogers or Abraham Maslow who follow this line.

To summarize this long chat about evidence: beware the extrapolators; check on the textbook or journal you are reading. What does the author regard as evidence? What does he neglect? What of his writing is fact and what is interpretation of fact?

Narrowing the field

Psychology is a big package. The scientific study of animal

and human behaviour is more than a 60-hour course. Psychology divides into many specialisms – developmental, industrial, clinical, social, occupational, educational, pastoral. The educational bit is your patch, though you will need to know a little about developmental, and the pastoral and educational may get pushed together in many school appointments. Since you hope to teach somebody something you will be interested in the psychology of learning processes, not just the learning of facts, but skills (social skills, manual skills, communication skills), attitudes and moral judgment. Even this is quite a formidable list, especially when you open it up to see what apparently simple learning processes involve. You soon find yourself wondering what facts are, and so get led on to considering concepts and how these are formed and developed. Much of it you will (I hope) find fascinating and sensible. Sometimes, almost on the side, you may feel anxieties or misgivings. The danger is that you will continually be knocking off from study to follow the misgivings down dark and misty alleys, so that you never understand what you're studying – and probably never solve the misgivings either. So it is well to look at two or three possible misgivings. and come to some sort of conclusion about them. You will then have a built-in 'death-to-red-herrings' mechanism which should make it at the very least much easier for you to get through your work. Misgivings come in a number of ways, especially for Christians:

1. Where is God in all this – especially if the learning might be something religious? Is it sensible to pray that your children will learn their RE especially quickly? Or, ought Christian children to learn more quickly than others? Part of the answer to this is along the lines of 'sustaining' or 'common' grace, outlined previously. In common with all general revelation, the laws of psychology are descriptions of the way God normally works in human life, just as the laws of physics or chemistry describe how God normally works in nature. So your study of learning processes is not something quite distinct from the rest of life. This is how God normally works. You may well believe that he does not always have to act in the normal way and so feel quite free to pray about the weather, a child's illness or tomorrow's lesson. You won't mind whether what happens is normal or a 'miracle'; both can be God's doing, God showing his care and control. The particular psychologist whose book you are reading may not have this perspective (any more than the meteorologist who explains the weather) but his description of what normally happens is worth following.

2. Isn't this all manipulation? I thought I was going to educate, in a relationship of care and love. Now it seems I am simply working a machine, providing stimulus and reinforcement; like a typist making lots of carbon copies, I press the right keys and the children know the right things. This is an inevitable result of analysis. We divide things up so that we can study them closely, without being distracted by other factors. So when you study learning processes you are, for the moment, cutting out questions concerning a child's pleasure in learning (except in so far as it is a reinforcement), the value to the child of what he learns, the truth of what he learns. You are studying, very narrowly, *how* he learns. This is not different in character from studying how to give an injection or persuade a crotchety old lady to take her medicine. Learning how can always be viewed as manipulation, in which case manipulation cannot always be bad. The driver of a one-man bus manipulates the passengers – he won't even let them sit down until they've paid! But this is perfectly right unless he charges the wrong fares. So the nurse's techniques are fine as long as it's the right injection and the right medicine. And your teaching techniques are fine as long as the right things are learned.

Or is it as simple as that? Suppose the old lady is fed up with living and doesn't want the medicine that might keep her alive; then you are faced with a discussion in the area of value and duty. And what is a nurse's responsibility regarding a patient's wishes and a patient's life? It certainly is not a problem of psychology. So the questions of *what* you should teach and *whether* you should teach someone who does not want to be taught are matters for discussion in other areas, not psychology. Deal with them sometime, but don't get them mixed up with the psychology. The particular problem of how the teaching of RE can be justified will be dealt with later (p. 113ff).

One further point arises here – a difference between teacher and nurse. As long as the medicine gets into the bloodstream of the patient all is well. It doesn't work quite like that for the teacher. 'Learning' does not mean just being able to repeat or reproduce information or technique. Usually there is some understanding involved. There would be no great evil in injecting children with the two-times table, or the first declension, but they ought also to understand what multiplication or inflexion is at some stage. Biblical psychology is particularly strong on this point. The Hebrew 'heart' is not an emotional term, but describes the centre of intelligent response, decision, moral direction, awareness. To act purely by appetite is less than human. To appeal only to appetite or instinct is to undervalue man's special quality as a thinking, responsible being. So Christians could not go along with a theory of learning (or instruction) which was concerned only to get the right behavioural responses irrespective of understanding. People can be drilled to kill or to pass an intelligence test without understanding either but it is gross manipulation of a bad kind. On the other hand many people remember with gratitude the teacher who made mathematics a life-long fascination, or literature a joy for them – manipulation of a good kind.

3. Where is truth in all this? There may be two sorts of truth. There is the truth of the evidence. Has the author found out something about the way people learn that matches the case? Then if you employ these techniques they will probably work. But this sort of truth has nothing

to do with whether what is taught is true or not. You may have a cast-iron technique for teaching children that $2 \times 3 = 7$; it may work every time. (More likely you will find cast-iron techniques for ensuring that children can't multiply at all!) But the truth or otherwise of $2 \times 3 = 7$ does not rest on the techniques by which it is communicated but on the logic of mathematics. Once again, keep *what* you teach separate from *how* you teach it. Indeed and alas, it is possible you will meet colleagues or lecturers whose pleasant and clear exposition of their views makes people think religion is unimportant; their communication skills are good; the content wrong. But this is only saying that teaching skills – or a stunning figure, or lots of money – are gifts that can be used for good or ill.

4. It's not very much like Sunday School. Many Christians who are training to be teachers have done their bit as Sunday School teachers. When they study the psychology of learning they begin to get red-faced about the way it was done in the old days. All this stuff about concept-formation makes you wonder if it was right to expect six-year-olds to understand atonement and regeneration; the findings on stimulus and reinforcement make you wonder if some children's evangelists go about things the right way. Probably you did your best as a Sunday School teacher and if things were wrong the blame may not have been yours but the superintendent's. (If you're still in touch with him you may have the tricky job of trying to update him.) It is also true to say that very many mothers and church teachers of young children do a marvellous job without knowing anything about concepts or connections – they tell stories, talk, sing, join in all sorts of rituals and play. A lot of Sunday School lesson material is available, much of it well edited by experienced teachers. On the other hand it must be said that the church has not always been good at teaching children and often treats them as mini-adults instead of growing people. It may fall to you sometime to help improve the methods and ideas in some church teaching, but it will need a lot of tact and care.

Unsettled areas

So much for general principles, matters that will affect your attitude towards the study of psychology in general. You will come across some areas where there is little agreement among the experts and different schools of thought dig in with more or less mutual suspicion and criticism. There will also be some areas where there is urgent need of a well-investigated Christian viewpoint, where Christians, by virtue of their experience and worldview, may have something to contribute apart from their broader involvement as human beings. Four areas are selected for comment.

1. Learning as mechanism

This was hinted at in connection with manipulation, but is worth comment on its own, since B. F. Skinner will figure prominently somewhere in your course. His very detailed experiments with animals produced results which have carried over into learning theory, particularly where the subject matter can be broken down into short, related items. Operant conditioning is the method whereby each successful bit of learning is rewarded, or reinforced, perhaps by food for animals, words of praise or gold stars for young children. Skinner is not interested in what goes on inside the child's mind (even if he allowed the word 'mind' at all). He is interested in behaviour modification in response to environment. His findings have been applied to many areas – teaching-machines, training of the mentally defective or autistic, programmed texts of all kinds (even one entitled *What makes a man a Christian?*). The extrapolators get busy and paint pictures of a society where there is complete conditioning. They have quite a few current instances in political mind-bending to make their prophecies scary. But the fact that learning takes place *this way* does not close the issue of *what* should be taught. Nor are we held in a vicious circle in which Skinner himself is the inevitable result of *his* learning experiences. Christians (and nonbelieving humans) can hold a doctrine of human responsibility and freedom which makes learning techniques one of the tools they use, choose to use, and should use responsibly. Skinner realizes there are two issues, though Jeeves (quoted above) is not happy with his answer:

'... it is not true to say ... that Skinner has failed to realise the importance of the question of, who controls the controller? Indeed, on p. 102 (*Beyond Freedom and Dignity*) he wrote,

"For whom is the powerful technology of behaviour to be used? Who is to use it? To what end? We have been implying the effects of one practice are better than those of another, but on what grounds? What is the good against which something else is better?" ...

Skinner has a simple, and as I would contend a simplistic and ethically naïve answer, namely that, "Survival is the only value according to which a culture is eventually to be judged and any practice that furthers survival, has survival value by definition."

In an almost unbelievable way the fact that the culture which survives may be tyrannical, bestial or brutal seems to be of no concern to Skinner. He writes, "What a given group of people call good is a fact: it is what members of the group find reinforcing as a result of their genetic endowment and the natural social contingencies to which they have been exposed. ..."

Skinner is a firm believer in what we may call *cultural relativism*, and, therefore, any suggestions that there are absolute revealed standards of right and wrong or good and evil is anathema to Skinner and his way of thinking. Here then is a clear conflict between Skinner's values and those of the Christian. But let us be quite clear that this conflict has nothing to do with scientific fact or scientific evidence. It is a matter of personal values which are not, in any way, logically tied to or derivable from Skinner's principles of learning or those of any other psychologist.'[6]

Once again, the 'machine' view is only one way of looking at man. It may make you horribly aware of the power one person can have over another for good or ill (as C. S. Lewis said: 'Man's control over nature always turns out to be one man's possibility of control over another').[7] But it does not make other complementary views wrong – we *can* decide and *are* responsible for deciding how we use the powers we learn about. And Christians believe that in this decision-making (and decision-implementing) we need not be alone, 'God is at work in you both to will and do his pleasure' (Phil. 2:13).

2. *Nature/Nurture*

An old problem that you may meet under different labels: genotype/phenotype or inheritance/environment. Everyone realizes the enormous influence of a child's surroundings; some 'don't have a chance', others have 'everything going for them'. It is no wonder that some middle class children are talking fluently and expressing a mature interest in everything when they start infant school, because their homes are full of colourful toys, books and pictures and their parents and siblings have been spending a lot of time with them (with or without the latest how-to-bring-up-your-child manual). On the other hand, every language has its proverbs about not being able to bring down what isn't in the attic, or purses and sows' ears.

There are three distinct questions in this: are there innate differences of ability? How can they be identified? What should we do about it? Keep the questions separate in your mind – it is possible that Christians will have something quite distinctive to say about the last one, but on the other two they must look for the answers in general revelation as with the physics and cookery. Unfortunately, the questions don't get separated very well. Jensen and Eysenck have been angrily refused a hearing by outraged students who regard them as élitist or racist and won't even give them a chance to report on their research. Extrapolators get busy again and paint pictures of eugenics gone mad *à la Brave New World* with a generation being bred to fit into a machine society. Eysenck himself specifically rejects the notion that education according to innate ability will make a more and more divided society; we must, he says, not disregard 'the importance of *regression*, the genetic factor which causes children of very bright and very dull parents to regress towards the mean of the whole population.'[8] Incidentally, it would not surprise Christians if God had built into the system somewhere a factor that set a boundary on men's selfish wish to organize things entirely their own way.

You may well think that research has concentrated too exclusively on innate differences of academic learning ability – verbal reasoning, spatial relationships and so on. Even Alfred Binet, the great-grandfather of all intelligence tests, said his tests 'cannot take account of elements of attention, will, popularity, teachability and courage ... Life is a struggle between characters, not a conflict of intellects.' It is more difficult (and therefore less often tried) to devise tests to see if there are innate differences of temperament, capacity to relate. Some work has been done on criminality, and much more on the inheritance of factors making for illness. Raymond Cattell is justly famous for his work on personality factor analysis. It is easy to take up an extreme position, especially if the third question gets mixed up with the other two. It is more responsible and sensible to try and get as accurate a view as possible about what differences do exist and what tests are appropriate to find them out.

Environment plays its part, too, and there is a welter of literature outlining research into how the psychological development of the child is influenced by home experience, especially in the earliest years. Again, some of this is mixed up with the researcher's own views about what ought to be done, but there is plenty to read and assess.

So you will eventually come to a reasonably informed position where you can start thinking about question three: what should be done about it? Parents can spend their income how they like (or can they?), so why not spend it on giving their children the very best possible education? Society needs clever people to run it (or does it?), so why not put a great proportion of national revenue to training clever children? Incidentally a quick look round the Annual Abstracts in the library will show the enormous disparity of provision under the present system between the (predominantly middle class) university undergraduate and the (predominantly working class) school leaver at 16. Should Christians have a definite view about this?

In very general terms it seems that the kingdom of God is on the side of justice, particularly the righting of imbalance between the powerful and weak. Widows, orphans, oppressed, depressed, get special attention in both Old and New Testaments. The Bible gives no egalitarian philosophy about everyone having equal right to wealth, health or happiness nor does it describe people as equal in potential. It does speak very clearly about equality in value to God and neighbour, of equality in sinnership, and equality in redeemability. How do these work out in discussion of specific issues? Streaming; mixed ability teaching; school structure; allocation of resources (the teaching of less able children in smaller sets); the allocation of special responsibility allowances: all these are things Christians urgently need to get working on. Central to the discussion will be the nature of the child, his individuality, his membership of a group. Joy James at an Association of Christian Teachers' conference has said we must never overlook

> 'the self-respect which preserves for teachers and others areas of individuality which children are not allowed to violate. There is also the child's respect for himself. Many learning problems arise from the child's loss of self-respect, the belief that he's not going to be able to learn, that he's no good. It is important that this respect

should be kept alive in the child. Teachers must foster it and never attempt to destroy it.'

It may seem a long way off, but teachers in training now will be the decision-makers of twenty years' time – as well as contributing a great deal in staff discussion in the meantime. How educational resources are divided within schools then may well depend on how you think about these things now.

3. Concept-formation

Here is another area which will occupy much of your course. Once again, you will find some divergence of opinion among the experts. It is a fascinating field of study, since one of the things about mankind seems to be his ability to think about things that aren't 'there'. As far as we can tell animals don't sit reflecting upon yesterday's experience, or the pleasure of meeting Gertie this evening; it is very unlikely they make generalizations about circles and triangles, or molecules, hormones, enzymes, or diminished fifth chords or iambic pentameters. Just how children come to make the generalizations, to arrive at a set of concepts, is an area of research you are bound to dip into. Piaget is the great name, but the sub-area of language-learning will introduce you to Chomsky and others. Language-learning is a particularly interesting study and gives the chance of comparing differing views of what the mind is like. Skinner's account of language (as learned response with all sorts of secondary reinforcements) is widely different from Chomsky's who believes man has linguistic aptitudes which cannot be investigated in animals.

Once again, separate the *how* from the *what* and *why*. Christians may well believe that the creation story of God breathing into man the breath of life so that he became a living soul (and Adam's words about Eve in Gn. 2:23, 'This at last is bone of my bone', not like the animals) would lead us to expect to find aptitude for learning and understanding that do not exist in animals. But we should still want to know *how* these aptitudes developed, under what stimuli, and at what stages. On the other hand, a psychologist telling us *how* these things arise does not empty them of value. For example, a psychology of how conscience develops in a young child does not mean we can disregard conscience, or that experiences of guilt have been explained away. You don't stop using your car just because you find out where it was made.

If you are doing a major piece of work on religious studies you will come up against Goldman's application of Piaget to the formation of religious concepts.[9] Once again the extrapolators have been hard at work saying that this has proved that the Bible is not a children's book, and painting horrific pictures of children who are exposed too young to Bible stories. If this crops up, make sure you look at the actual research questions Goldman used, in conjunction with a critical review. It has important consequences for religious teaching, but not in the sweeping way that is often represented. Joy James says bluntly,

> 'Whether or not the Bible is taught in school depends very much on society's verdict on the truth of the Bible. It does not depend upon any consideration of the psychology of learning. By the age of six, society has decided (quite arbitrarily), children should be well on their way to understanding in three areas of abstract learning: first of all speech ... secondly, written language ... thirdly, the mathematical area of knowledge.'

Although Piaget is still held in high honour, it is widely agreed he has not given the complete blue-print. There is still a lot of work to be done on the question of concept-formation. Christians are in the concept business in a big way – especially articulate, educated Christians who verbalize easily and throw ideas about with aplomb. All those late-night discussions about predestination, charismata and inspiration need more conceptualization than even the participants may have. So Christians of all people ought to be concerned about if, how and when young children of various abilities and backgrounds can form abstract concepts like God, myself, forgiveness, guilt, love, or moral concepts of right, consideration, sympathy. We may need to distinguish more sharply between forming a concept and being able to express it verbally – and this means more attention to testing techniques. We may also have to ask whether differences of intellectual level affect ability (or need) to arrive at sophisticated concepts. Perhaps we have overrated the *ordering* of experience and underrated the *experiencing* – naïve enjoyment may be more important then being able to classify the experience correctly.

4. Sanctified discontent

What can one person do? The time for study is short. Problems come thick and fast. There are some old ones sharpened up a little; some new ones staring you in the face for the first time. Every now and then you feel bursting within you a question that seems so hopelessly naïve and basic that you can't bring yourself to express it. Surely it must be a silly question since no one ever asks it. Perhaps people don't ask it because they are afraid of it, or because they know nothing can be done about it. The question is: why do we pay such enormous homage to intellectual ability? Why, for instance, does so much effort go on teaching people *things,* facts, skills, academic manipulation? Why is society so slanted towards the people with paper qualifications? Why is examination work in secondary schools reckoned to be 'easier' than non-examination things like general studies, social studies, general R.E.? Why are tutor groups regarded by so many children (and staff) as a waste of time?

You may never ask these questions – especially if you are training for secondary, and if your own education was peacefully academic and 'successful'. It would be better if you did ask some of them. We have invested so much time, resource and research into academic types of learning – possibly because it is easier to measure results, possibly because there is more agreement on what counts as 'right'. We need more thought and research about how we give children an insight into the worth of other developments of personality. If this means surprising some parents, then we have a job of parent education on our hands too. It may mean surprising some well established teachers – and comprehensive reorganization has already jolted many well established, academic teachers into thinking about the three-quarters of the population they used not to see. You may be overwhelmed by the size of the problem and despair of doing anything about it, but it is better to keep alive an attitude of sanctified discontent. Do not lose the vision of children as more than examination material. Children of all abilities can stand and stare, wonder, worship, rejoice, share warm and caring relationship far beyond anything they can analyse or describe. If we are truly educators and not just instructors, then this is part of our patch and Christians ought to be in the forefront of any move to cultivate it.

It is possible that your psychology studies will make you wonder if learning techniques are not being used all too successfully by consumer industries to make people want things rather than personal experience. There is truth in much of what is said about the country's need of engineers and technicians; that wealth-producers are needed to pay the wages of the rest of us. Careers lessons and counselling are right to put children realistically in the picture about what jobs there are and where the rewards are. But an industrial society, wedded to export booms and high internal consumption, is not necessarily what the kingdom of God stands for. Home-making may well (even on economic terms) turn out in the long run to be more productive of wealth and security than an 'economically active' career.

1 H. J. Eysenck, *The Inequality of Man* (Fontana, 1975).
2 M. Jeeves, *Spectrum,* Vol. 8 no. 2, 1976.
3 M. Jeeves, *Spectrum,* Vol. 8 no. 2, 1976.
4 ed. M. J. Taylor, *Progress and Problems in Moral Education* (NFER, 1975).
5 G. Ryle, *The Concept of Mind* (Penguin, 1963).
6 M. Jeeves, *Spectrum,* Vol. 8 no. 2, 1976.
7 C. S. Lewis, *The Abolition of Man* (Geoffrey Bles, 1946).
8 H. J. Eysenck, *The Inequality of Man*, p. 188.
9 R. Goldman, *Readiness for Religion* (Routledge & Kegan Paul, 1965).

7. Applications

The philosophy, sociology and psychology of education that you study seem a long way removed from what will actually occupy you for the thousand hours a year that Burnham think you will work. You may be cutting notches in the doorpost or otherwise marking off the days till you get at the 'real thing'. You will of course be observing and even doing some teaching on T.P. You may be fortunate enough to do this in schools where the staff welcome you, explain and let you get on with it in just the right proportions, and don't regard you as an inevitable disaster after whom they will have to spend a week clearing up. Some schools will actually try and explain how what they do is related to the theory you have been studying. You might never guess unless they told you, but it is worth spending time thinking out principles underlying practice. There will not be a lot of time for this sort of thinking when you are starting in the full-time job, so spare a thought now for some of the major applications. Once again, notice how the presuppositions people start with influence the schemes they end up with.

Authority and discipline

One of the difficulties of changing from student to teacher is that you have at some stage to jump over the fence from the field of those who traditionally push against authority into the field of those who traditionally exert authority. Maybe you were a school prefect (if your school had such things), and have never been among the more vociferous minority who get students such a protesting and ill-disciplined image. Even so, you do not necessarily see it as part of your present calling to support the management and silence all criticism. When you are in post as a teacher you will not necessarily agree with all that the management do, but you will be inescapably identified with authority, and certainly trying to keep what you regard as reasonable discipline among children.

Some presuppositions don't get you very far here. Existentialists are all for the individual doing his own thing. Authority and discipline are part of the 'conventions' which deny authentic existence and squeeze everyone into a mould. Of course there may be limits. The most existentialist art teacher may welcome a pupil who wants to create patterns by throwing paint at the wall, but will hesitate if pupil first wants to stand teacher in front of wall and see what pattern is left after the paint-throwing. Existentialists are good in protest, good at urging commitment and reality, but not good at building structures in which commitment and reality can be lived out.

Similarly the extreme man-is-a-machine or man-is-an-animal presuppositions lead to a machine or farm model of school. Authority is necessary because well-structured groups have more chance of survival. The way you discipline will be dictated by behaviourist considerations — sticks and carrots. You may meet the occasional hard-headed old hand (or even youngster, since teaching seems to make fascists of all ages) who acts as if this were so. Rewards and punishments have kept his form quiet and examination results passable for years, and that's the best tip he can give you.

These extremes account for relatively few of the teaching profession. Many more would follow the intuition lobby (must have law and order; kids know it too, really); the utilitarian 'It's best for everybody', with a fair admixture of reason (the concept of education involves the concept of order and discipline).

A Christian can accept all these as saying something true about the situation, but none as the only or complete key. God's care for mankind (and children in particular) is shown partly in the general revelation that order and structure are essential for the world to work smoothly. By the same token, children may not need to be able to explain the concept of authority before they can respond to reasonable authority. Teachers need to work at the concept, however, to make sure they are not simply accepting, uncritically, slick answers to keep the kids quiet. 'I'm in charge here' is a good slogan only if you know what being in charge means. It needs a careful bit of analysis.

First, distinguish authority from power. Power means you can get things done whether you ought to or not. Authority means you have the right to get (some) things done, whether you have the power or not. Power without authority is dangerous. Authority without power is pathetic to watch and worse to experience. Authority must be ready to justify itself and listen to criticism. Power usually disregards criticism.

Secondly, distinguish various sorts of authority. There is an authority that comes from appointment – this involves being responsible *for* something or someone *to* someone. This is part of a teacher's authority – you are society's delegate in looking after 4C. There is an authority that comes from ability – the sole map-reader among a party of lost hikers has authority to lead. Part of a teacher's authority comes from expertise and children quickly recognize that you *do* know the skill or subject you are trying to teach them. The subject, in a way, exercises its authority over you, too – you *can't* let them write rubbish without correction. There is also an authority that arises from personality – a charismatic quality that commands respect. This is a bit less easy to keep in its place. Perhaps a charismatic teacher may be giving slanted lessons, which children lap up because of her commanding personality.

Appointment is open to test (you can check what the teacher was appointed to do); expertise is open to test (you can check whether he is teaching the right stuff). Ultimately authority from appointment can be traced by a Christian back to God – it is part of the 'authority' which God intends should characterize human society (Rom. 13:1–7); authority from expertise can be traced back to God, the author of all truth. Perhaps charisma could be traced back to God's giving or call.

So for the Christian there is an anchorage for what goes on in the classroom. He is part of a chain that links the children to the reality of life; something given, not invented; something to which both teacher and child (at their differing levels) are subject. Teachers who do not share your Christian belief may still be in favour of reasonable authority, but won't go right back to your presupposition of God as anchor-man. They will start somewhere lower down – perhaps with a secularized version of Romans 13 which says you must have a firm framework for society to function properly; perhaps joined with a common sense view that 'you know what you're talking about' and this gives you the right to pass it on. All such will agree (as against extreme individualists) that school must have structure and a study must have means of assessment. Just why this should be so is the subject of some disagreement – from Hobbes who thought mankind put up with administration because anarchy was worse, to Rousseau and more sophisticated forms of social contract.

Such frameworks need maintaining; such study needs persistence. So discipline arises as necessary in social and academic learning. Again differing presuppositions give differing answers. The behaviourist will soon find out what stimuli provoke the responses he wants – in cruder days this even amounted to 'making an example of the first to step out of line, to show the rest who's in charge' (*i.e.*, reducing the offending *person* to the role of *thing*, visual aid). At the other extreme are a few teachers who dislike discipline because they believe children to be basically good and creative, and that a fixed pattern of behaviour or learning might repress them. Most teachers occupy a (mildly muddled) middle position, appealing to reason, social conscience, self-interest, and relying on whatever charisma they have and whatever interest the subject can engender. The biblical emphasis is heavily on justice and equality (which is what reason turns out to be in practice) and also on care. You discipline because you care for the child, not just to make things easy for yourself ('I never have any trouble in *my* lessons' is only part commendation). So praise or blame must take account of the child's performance in the context of the child's background. Structure and routine must be appropriate to abilities. Of course biblical references are mostly about *moral* education, the formation of character, but curriculum development and teaching method can never be seen entirely apart from the 'hidden curriculum' and the values and attitudes it stands for. In any case it is nonsense to suppose that character formation can be timetabled in moral education or social studies lessons and left at that. Every teacher is passing on some idea of what is socially acceptable or worth following. Christian teachers would try both to hold an offender responsible and at the same time show understanding and concern for him as a person, with the memory that Jesus managed to do both and never despaired of anyone. Modern theories of punishment (if any) emphasize the deterrent value, the reforming value, but often leave out the element of retribution. The first two are open to 'machine' considerations, anything that 'works' being acceptable. The third must take account of what is just, not only what 'works'.

Parents' rights, pupils' rights

These may seem very different but are put together because they both run into the difficulty of talking about rights. It is not just word-splitting fussiness to say that whenever any parent, child (or teacher) says 'I know my rights!' they are probably telling a factual untruth and philosophically confused. Even at the level of what statute law says, the situation is not clear. You may have heard the phrase 'as confident as a barrister on a zebra crossing' and much the same could be said about parents or pupils making a case to the education authorities.

Theologically, the question is even more difficult. The Bible has little to say about rights, but a lot to say about authority, duty and responsibility. Incidentally, in the course of the emphasis upon authority, duty and responsibility, those sections of society most liable to oppression get powerful support. The prophets do not speak of the poor farmer's right to justice in the gate, but to the judgment of God against those who twist evidence and use false weights. The widow and fatherless in the Psalms who plead for 'judgment' or 'justice' are not asking for *their* rights, but that what *is* right should be done, and that God should do it. The distinction may seem subtle, but is well worth pondering.

You will often hear people who carry responsibility (including teachers) complaining that 'everyone seems more concerned about their rights than their duties nowadays'. On the other hand you may have skimmed through enough social and economic history to know that if some energetic folk had not championed the rights of half the British population, exploitation and poverty would be even worse than they are. The particular problem of the present time is the lack of any presupposition that will stand the weight of a superstructure of rights. The American Declaration of Independence appealed to self-evidence: 'We hold these truths to be self-evident, that all men are created equal, that they are endowed by their Creator with certain inalienable rights, that among these are life, liberty and the pursuit of happiness.' But as society gets less and less sure that there is any creator, it is harder and harder to find anywhere to anchor fundamental rights. So, for example, *Children's Rights* by Paul Adams and others[1], for all its discussion and indignation, nowhere gives a philosophy of rights; the writers expect you to agree that the anomalies they expose are stupid and the solutions they propose are common sense. *Parent Power* edited by Nicholas Bagnall[2] is an excellent summary of the law, but does not attempt to ground the law in anything deeper. In fact, it is often critical of the law – as, for example, about *in loco parentis*: 'It's a key phrase which assumes that the relationship between a child and his teachers is the same as that between a child and his parents. It's probably wrong, but it's the law.' If the law is 'wrong' you must be putting it alongside a 'right' standard which can be supported by other means, but Bagnall does not attempt to say what this is. It appears as if common sense is going to have to do the job again: 'Legally, parents have very little power when it comes to the education of their children ... In practice, though, parents have great power ...' and this power turns out to involve persuasion, reasoning, explaining, talking with teachers, heads, administrators who will in the end 'see reason'. The law itself seems to put money on reason, as everything is to be done as a 'reasonable parent' would do it. Section 68 of the 1944 Education Act lays down that '... pupils are to be educated in accordance with the wishes of their parents' (it doesn't say why; laws never say why) but only in so far as is 'compatible with the provision of efficient instruction and training and the avoidance of unreasonable public expenditure'. A test case in 1966 elucidated the fact that 'unreasonable expenditure' had more weight than parents' wishes in the case of a parent who didn't want Johnny to go to the local comprehensive. On the other hand Section 68 gives parents the right of appeal to the Secretary of State but only if the local authority is acting 'unreasonably'.

If you have a 'machine' set of presuppositions, then society works by rules which evolve to give maximum efficiency – whate'er is best administered is best. Parents come into the picture only to produce children at school gates at 9 am, collect them at 3.30 pm and keep them fed and clothed. The teacher works out what is the most efficient curriculum for filtering children at the end into the tasks that will keep the social machine running.

Argument based on 'animal' or 'social animal' presuppositions is much the same, though the emphasis on survival may be clearer. So Robert Ollendorf: 'Nevertheless, it must be possible to deduce a living principle, a "truth" underlying the history of human societies, because otherwise the human race would have failed to survive at a very early stage.'[3]

The 'reason' brigade start off from apparently strong ground. If children are to be treated differently from anyone else – and if different children are to be treated differently from each other – then there must be something to justify the difference of treatment. There must be some relevant difference of situation. The case is closely argued in J. P. White's *Towards a Compulsory Curriculum*.[4] Any compulsory schooling at all is a constraint upon children; a compulsory curriculum even more so. So if education (or anything else) is said to 'act in the general interest at the expense of the individual's, then it must be able to justify this' (p. 7). He claims that certain activities can be justified on the ground that they are 'worthwhile' (in the sense described by R. S. Peters[5]) and that children must be acquainted with them if they are to be able to make an open choice of how to direct their lives. How they choose is up to them, but they cannot choose unless someone, at some time, has given them the material upon which to choose – whether they liked it or not. Parents are among those who 'know what is good' for children; so are teachers. Both (according to those who base the case on 'reason') should teach children what they need to be able to make their own rational choices, and should then respect the choices made. There will be cases where you find yourself as a teacher working happily with parents, agreeing on what is worthwhile and good for the children. You may find children agreeing too. On the other hand you will often find yourself differing from parents who either reject your educational vision, or else see it as *the* way to push and shove Johnny willy-nilly into the élite. And you will almost certainly find the articulate adolescent who wants to argue his rights against both of you.

The following extract from Barry Palmer[6] is worth thinking over to see the sort of context in which a Christian world-view sets the matter:

> 'In the birth and growth to maturity of every child we see the continuing work of God as Creator. This activity is complete only when the mature individual lives in a loving and productive relationship with the natural world, with human society, and with God. It is thus always partially impeded under the conditions of our existence.
>
> God carries out this work through human agents, that is, those who bring children into the world, feed, protect, rear, and educate them. They are thus not *our* children, whether we are parents or teachers, but God's children. Kahlil Gibran's words express a basically Christian viewpoint. "Your children are not your children ... They come through you but not from you, and though they are with you yet they do not belong to you. You may give them your love but not your thoughts, for they have their own thoughts. You may house their bodies but not their souls, for their souls dwell in the house of tomorrow, which you cannot visit, not even in your dreams."
>
> Whether the child's home environment consists of a large extended family, two parents, a mother, or an institution, God uses this environment, within its limitations, for the fulfilment of His creative purposes. He uses it whether the persons concerned are believers or unbelievers

Through this early experience the child forms his basic ideas about himself, and about those upon whom one depends. This is therefore the groundwork for his understanding of the character of God as Father, upon which any teaching he subsequently receives will be built.

As he grows older others including teachers continue this parental function. It is important for him that what they do is correlated with what has been learned through his home. Otherwise he is split between conflicting authorities, and may grow up divided in himself, or be forced to repudiate either his home or his education. ...

The teacher is an agent of God in His work as Ruler, as well as in His work as Creator. He is an agent of the community and of social policy, dealing with children *en bloc* as well as individually. The teacher's role therefore involves him in sustaining the tension between these two commitments, to the individual child and to the community. If he is a Christian he needs to consider how God is working through both the creating and ruling aspects of his role.'

Authority and rights: a postscript.

In both the above matters – which are really the same area looked at from two sides – there is a distinction to be made. Some teachers will tell you that all the clever theoretical stuff is a waste of time. However you theorize, you've got to do what the school rules, or LEA, or head of department says. You can think what you like as long as you do what I say! This highlights the age-old discussion between natural law and positive law. Positive law is what actually happens; the law as it is enacted and enforced in a particular community – traffic laws, commercial laws, laws of libel, laws about comprehensive organization, regulations about British Summer Time; dates of holidays; and, in a slightly less grandiose manner, the rules of Alderman Muggins Infant-Junior School or the Slagville High School. These at least give you a place to start from; a framework to live in. As the old sweats will tell you, it's job enough enforcing that lot, without theorizing any further.

But the time will inevitably come when someone will want to challenge some of the positive law. Perhaps, not long ago, they were met with stonewalling. Why must I wear a tie? Because that's what the uniform regulations say. End of discussion. Often, however, even the most positive of lawyers deign to give some further reason – you mustn't wear high-heeled shoes to school because you might trip on the open stairs in the tower block, to the danger of yourself and others. But more seriously, there are cases where you want to challenge school rules, or LEA regulations, or even national laws on the ground that they are 'unfair'. Here you are appealing from positive law to natural law.

Natural law has a long history, from Sophocles' *Antigone* 'th' unalterable, unwritten law of heaven ... that cometh none knows whence', through Stoics, mediaeval Christianity and Locke to the 20th century human rights movement. Christians would see it as the expression of the 'law in their hearts' of Romans 2. Calvin wrote of conscience which 'instead of allowing us to stifle our perception, and sleep on without interruption, acts as an inward witness and monitor, reminds us of what we owe to God, points out the distinction between good and evil. ...'[7] Natural law is making a modest come-back after a time in the wilderness. It fell on hard times in the 19th century, mainly at the hands of Jeremy Bentham who described it as 'Rhetorical nonsense, nonsense upon stilts', and claimed that only positive law was any use. Of course he had a point. It is not much cheer to a maimed political prisoner in Chile, Russia or South Africa to know that Article 5 of the Universal Declaration of Human Rights says 'No one shall be subjected to torture or to cruel, inhuman or degrading treatment or punishment'; nor to the railwayman, dismissed for failure to belong to a trade union, to know that Article 20(2) says 'No one may be compelled to belong to an association.' What matters is not what theorists *say* ought to happen, but what actually happens. You will certainly experience this tension in your teaching career. What's the use of spending time thinking what ought to be done, when you know the head and top brass won't hear of any change from the present (possibly unjust) practice? First, of course, you must find out what ways are open to you of altering what happens now. Persuasion, sweet reasonableness, a little gentle lobbying may yield some results and may well be within the 'structures for negotiation' that exist already. It could be that differences will be so fundamental that you have to move. This would be a rare case, though I suspect quite a bit of movement in the teaching profession reflects unhappiness with structures and attitudes as much as desire for promotion or wider experience. In less serious situations what usually happens is that the concerned teacher finds ways of tempering justice with mercy. The rules are minima. They do not limit what can be done in other ways to help and heal. You may be obliged to enforce rules against truancy, rudeness and such like, but this need not inhibit you from going on to find out the conditions and reasons behind the behaviour, and perhaps to offer what help you can.

Thinking about it is certainly not a waste of time – nor discussing it with other people. At least, knowing what ought to be done (even if you don't do it) is a stage further than not knowing (or being convinced that what is done now is right).

Co-operation and community

Schools have always said a lot about co-operation. It has not only been lip-service on speech days to 'working together to build this community of which we can be justly proud …'. It has been a very real feature of relationships between staff, and between many staff and many pupils. The rise of large schools, and schools of wider ability range, has focused even more attention upon community. Year heads, house heads, counsellors, co-ordinators of one sort and another all see part of their job as 'building up a community'. In some areas the community extends outside the immediate area of the school, and we have community schools where parents and neighbours use the building for classes in the evening (and sometimes in the day, too). Some schools have community teachers who visit homes and local caring agencies and provide liaison with the school. In a church school this might perhaps be built upon a strong sense of community in the parish. What should a Christian teacher think about this emphasis on community? How does he co-operate in it with people who do not share (or even respect) his faith?

First consider what you might share quite honestly with non-Christian teachers. Colleagues may not use the biblical words to describe these six areas, but may well agree with the points made.

(i) 'He made from one every nation of men ...' (Acts 17:26). There is *a basic unity*; racial, physical, intellectual differences should not bar anyone from the community (unless necessary for their specialist, separate help as with, *eg.*, ESN).

(ii) 'You cause grass to grow for cattle and plants for man to cultivate that he may bring forth fruit from the earth' (Ps. 104:14). The world is there to be used responsibly. The layout of the mediaeval village suggested some sense of community rooted in the soil. The common dependence upon the mystery of growth, togetherness in plenty or famine, was evident in a way unknown in chrome-plated supermarkets, or in tower blocks which separate people from the earth and each other. Many teachers, Christian or not, agree that this sense of responsible use of the earth, and a sense of common dependence and community, is a worthy educational objective.

(iii) 'They show that what the law requires is written on their hearts' (Rom. 2:15). There is enough underlying moral awareness to make community a matter of shared standards, mutual consideration for truth and care.

(iv) 'Train up a child according to his way' (Pr. 22:6). There is something given about each individual, a temperament and ability that must be respected. We may well find some temperaments uncongenial, but must learn to live with them, and give them opportunity to develop in the context of the community.

(v) 'Let everyone be subject ...' (Rom. 13:1). There are relationships of government and administration which are essential to any community. There must be structure. Rousseau may see it as the result of social contract; Hobbes as the inevitable fruit of human selfishness. The New Testament sees it as part of God's providence, giving people somewhere secure to grow. It may well be part of education to help children develop sound criticism of existing institutions, but to sow doubts that *any* institution is necessary is to unman them.

(vi) 'He has set eternity in their hearts' (Ec. 3:11). Children (and grown-ups if not denatured) share a sense of wonder and quest. It is no good saying that such questions are unanswerable and useless. Every generation asks sooner or later 'Who am I?'. 'What is the purpose of life?' Why is the world so beautiful, so perplexing, so full of suffering?' 'What is after death?' All these building blocks for community are shared widely by thinking people. Rooted in them, a community may prosper and develop personal and interpersonal richness. Schools often succeed better than many of the larger communities that surround them in building upon these foundations and teachers of all faiths and none co-operate in the building. But Christians are also committed to say that mankind shares two other things, less popularly understood and often less welcome.

(vii) 'All the world is subject to the judgment of God' (Rom. 3:19). There is a bias to wrong, recognized by Ovid and Huxley as well as Paul. 'The good that I would, I do not'. More seriously, the Bible does not even leave it at that but talks of a still deeper unity. Men are not only united by being *for* themselves, but for themselves *against* God. There is no difference for all have sinned, and this root reluctance to 'glorify God as God' is man's widest and most pressing problem.

(viii) The good news of the gospel is that all men share a possibility of redemption and renewal. Self-centredness gives way to God-centredness and concern for others. Again 'there is no difference, the same Lord over all is rich towards all who call upon him' (Rom. 10:12).

Christians cannot deny their understanding of the last two points, but must (and would want to) co-operate with others who share the rest. We cannot accept the pessimism of the man-is-only-animal writers who dismiss community as merely a useful aid to survival. Nor can we sweep all willy-nilly into the kingdom of God. What we have to do is to work out what *is* shared in the communities we try to build; what flaws there may be and what tools we share to mend them. We may rejoice in God's good giving to all, but still bear witness to his special goodness in the redemption of the world, the means of grace and the hope of glory. This is a position of tension and we might prefer to be either prophets of doom declaring woe upon the whole show, or to withdraw altogether. But if God calls us to work in schools – which are a microcosm of the real world, with real, sinful but redeemable people – then we must try to work out the whole of our faith.

A newcomer, to make co-operation and community into a trio, is 'consensus'. 'Seeking a consensus' seems to be a major preoccupation of chairmen of committees, leaders of working parties, and even head teachers in staff meetings. Like all good gifts around us, the idea may be misused. The move towards co-operation and community is a welcome change from the autocracy and regimentation of some earlier times and places.

Consensus followed unobtrusively. You must, after all, *agree* to co-operate and *agree* broadly what community you are trying to make. Indeed some of the shared factors are given above. But a shared *recognition* of some basic facts and aims does not mean that a majority is always right. Consensus came in to sojourn and must needs be a judge, and we hear all too often of an idea having 'general support' as though that made it right. The 'climate of modern opinion' carries about as much moral weight as the 'millions of housewives' who 'can't be wrong' in the soap-powder advert. If consensus meant the 'waiting upon God' which the early Quakers practised until they arrived at the 'way of peace', it would be well worth respecting. All too often, it means persuading, re-drafting, compromising, cajoling, until all but the most recalcitrant agree reluctantly that the proposed solution is 'the best in the circumstances'. There is certainly a place for the honest broker who discusses and trades viewpoints with various parties to a discussion, but the desire to reach a formula with which everyone agrees is a dark temptation. Often it results in a decision so watery that it meets no serious facet of the case; also it may leave deep suspicion and resentment beneath the superficial 'agreement'. Philosophically, of course, it is nonsense to suppose that popular agreement makes anything 'true'. History has often been made by the lonely martyr of conscience who has followed truth *contra mundum*.

On the other hand, don't be too ready to put yourself forward as martyr-elect. Co-operation and community don't demand that you agree to everything that is said or done. They do demand that you make your own views clear, that you accept the decision of those whose job it is to make decisions (after consultation), subject to whatever safeguards of individual conscience there may be available. Consensus tends to invoke an eleventh commandment: thou shalt not rock the boat. But a firm community and sense of co-operation can survive, and even thrive upon, a little gentle boat-rocking done in the right spirit. So when decisions have to be made about reorganization, or mixed ability grouping, or set books in CSE English, you should be able, with courtesy and clarity, to make your contribution to discussion. When the decision is made, you should be able to co-operate with integrity in making it work. You don't have to pretend you agree. You don't even have to keep on saying you disagree.

Is RE 'indoctrination'?

A little was said earlier (p. 93) about Goldman's application of Piaget's theories of learning to RE. This attracted a lot of publicity at the time, though as Joy James comments, 'Whether or not the Bible is taught in school depends very much on society's verdict on the truth of the Bible ... not upon any consideration of the psychology of learning.' This is an area where public opinion depends very much on which 'public' you ask. The general public, beloved of Gallup pollsters, persist in calling themselves Christians, don't go to church, want their children taught RE. The general opinion among teachers and those who have experienced a liberal higher education is that RE is a tricky subject, possibly even dangerous, with the main danger being indoctrination. A report in the late 70s by the National Secular Society spoke with some glee of 'affixing the label of Indoctrination to Religious Education' and certainly many teachers – even convinced Christian teachers – are sensitive on this issue. If RE is one of your major studies then obviously you must sort this question out. If not, it will still be good to have an answer in draft. The discussion involved will help sort out significant principle from acquired prejudice.

Indoctrination is a relatively recent arrival on the list of educational swear-words. 'I teach, thou instructest, he indoctrinates ... they brainwash'. A cynic might say that 'teaching' means passing on knowledge I agree with and 'indoctrinating' means passing on knowledge I disagree with. But this is not the whole story. It is true that 'indoctrinate' has become a swear-word in the last few years, at a time when religious belief has been under attack. But during those same years the whole process of teaching has been under scrutiny with great emphasis on the need for *understanding*. The rote-learning of facts and second-hand opinions gives way to greater opportunity for finding out facts and forming judgments about them. There still has to be a good deal of 'telling them', especially with younger children, but the aim is to bring them to a level of understanding where they can see for themselves why what they have been told should be accepted. The mistake lies in assuming that all indoctrination is bad. Either save 'indoctrination' to mean 'wrong use of instructional techniques' or else qualify it with 'good' or 'bad'. Good indoctrination could then include all the socialization that goes on in the average primary school, leading up to the time when children *understand* how to live with other people. Bad indoctrination could include biased lessons that deliberately present only one side of a case, or any remaining examples of the practice whereby schools put pupils in for confirmation because 'everyone in your year gets confirmed'.

Unhappily I fear indoctrination is lumbered with bad vibrations, so the best we can do is to show that it is unavoidable, or that RE is no worse than any other subject in this respect. The standard summary on the subject is still Professor Basil Mitchell's addendum to the Durham Report.[8] He examines three areas which are very briefly summarized below. (The whole paper is well worth careful study.)

Method 'A indoctrinates B in respect of p (a belief) if A brings it about that B believes p otherwise than enabling B to understand the reasons for p.' It is easy to show this happens in all teaching, however much the object may be to lead pupils to eventual understanding of as much truth as possible.

Content This emphasis tries to limit indoctrination to apply only where the subject matter 'is a debatable or controversial statement', but Mitchell shows that this still leaves a very wide field under any indoctrination ban, including many areas that the most liberal humanist would want to teach.

Aims Indoctrination is now said to be related to the aim that B believes p 'in such a way that he is unable subsequently to be believe not-p, even if presented with sufficient reasons for believing not-p'. This would amount to giving a pupil a closed mind in certain areas, and this would be universally rejected.

But what about aiming to convey a strong acceptance, so that pupils would be prepared to look at contrary evidence, but to look very carefully and suspiciously? Mitchell answers with an argument first noted by Burke, which is worth quoting at some length:

'1. The liberal ideal of the wholly autonomous rational individual ... cannot be realised. Every individual grows to maturity in a cultural tradition and cannot produce a rational 'philosophy' of his own from scratch.

2. It is not only false but dangerous for the individual to *think* he is capable of doing this. Society depends for its proper functioning upon a multiplicity of shared beliefs, values and attitudes, and will suffer ... if the individual feels that these have no claim upon him except in so far as he can independently validate them.

3. To the extent that these shared beliefs, *etc.*, are eroded by 'rational' criticism, their place in the life of the individual and society will be taken not by beliefs that are based upon good reasons, but by ideas that are largely the product of current fashion. Educators who scrupulously refrain from introducing any bias into the educational process will not thereby ensure that their pupils escape bias, only that the bias is imparted by other agencies.'

After ten years' flirtation with 'neutrality' it is now much more widely agreed that a teacher cannot avoid – and indeed should have – commitments of his own. He should be committed to his subject, its content and methods; he should be committed to certain standards of personal and professional behaviour. These commitments are part of the evidence he takes into the classroom with him; whether he wishes or not, they will show through his presentation and personality. It is right that they should and, if challenged, that he should state them with whatever comment is appropriate. All that is necessary is that he should acknowledge opposite viewpoints and not cause his pupils to believe that his own commitment is other than a *commitment*. Edward Hulmes, Director of Farmington Institute for Christian Studies, comments:

> 'It is reassuring to know that openness does not exclude commitment, if this is taken to mean the finding of truth by the individual. To the extent that the teacher has himself been involved in this process of seeking and finding he will be entitled, and indeed obliged, to use his commitment *explicitly* as a primary teaching resource. For the moment it can be said that the declaration of personal commitment, not as a constantly repeated routine, but with sufficient emphasis to make it clear (and not only after children have asked for it) is one of the surest ways by which any teacher can avoid indoctrinating those whom he teaches.'[9]

The discussion may have done some good in making both believers and unbelievers aware of how much they do 'indoctrinate' and in sifting out what is valid from what is not. There may have been Christian teachers who fostered uncritical belief, and liberal lecturers who kept students away from belief by lampooning 'fundamentalists'. Perhaps both are now more ready to present a courteously reasoned case and to respect the integrity of the hearer, yet without pretending to be neutral.

All this has to do with the concept of indoctrination and might apply to RE, history, art, literature or politics. A few words specifically about RE might also be useful. The Durham Report, already referred to, is a mine of information. It argues throughout that RE must be included in the curriculum on educational grounds, not because Britain is a 'Christian country',[10] not because public opinion at any time seems to favour it, not because RE is the basis of morality, but because it is an essential area of knowledge with an important contribution to make to general education. This educational justification is the one most frequently made and most widely accepted. Church, Bible class, school voluntary group, may all have, as their aim, introducing people to personal faith in Christ and helping them to grow in that faith. Such cannot be the aim of a school in a secular state system. But it is a proper aim of a secular state school that pupils should have a sympathetic understanding of the religious view of life which has characterized most of its history and the history of the world and still motivates many of its citizens. Not to include such information and understanding is, in fact, a powerful form of negative indoctrination, because it gives the impression that such things are not as important as those others included in the curriculum. This educational justification is developed in a recent leaflet prepared by the Avon RE Resources Centre, Bristol, which says:

> 'RE has a unique role in giving the pupil a more sensitive understanding of other people and a deeper knowledge of himself ... a number of skills which, collectively, make up the distinctive contribution of the subject to the school curriculum. The following is not an exhaustive list, but indicates some of the skills which RE tries to develop:
> – ability to handle and interpret different kinds of evidence (historical, sociological and textual)

- ability to use different methods of enquiry (reading, observation and reflection)
- ability to grasp the meaning of unfamiliar, and often quite difficult, ideas and concepts
- ability to deal with a large body of information and to select what is important and relevant
- imagination and sensitivity in seeking to understand the beliefs and attitudes of others.
- awareness of the factors influencing one's own attitudes and judgments.'

All this of course will leave open the question of content. Should Christianity be the main content of British schools' RE teaching? Most agreed syllabuses include material about other religions though it is increasingly recognized that it is impossible to do justice to them all. The Lancaster Schools Council Project tries to solve the matter phenomenologically by looking at particular phenomena – things religious people *do* – and this is a useful entry to further study.

In areas with large minority groups, an understanding of the significance of the ritual of other religions is valuable, even essential, from primary school onwards, but attempts to 'do Hinduism' in half-a-dozen lessons are beyond almost all teachers and most non-Hindu children. The short time usually allowed for RE makes any attempt to do justice to major world faiths unrealistic, even if teachers had the expertise. There is sound sense in trying to give a solid understanding of the dominant historical belief – that is, in Britain, Christianity – so that pupils have some base from which to work in understanding whatever other religious expression they may meet. For much of the compulsory school age pupils are taught (in all subjects) material that is presented as worthy of acceptance. At the same time they are progressively taught skills of criticism and analysis appropriate to the subject. So in RE there must be a steady input of accepted material along with growing skills to weigh and assess rival truth-claims. In an important lecture ('Teaching religion in a secular plural society') Bishop Lesslie Newbigin comments:

> 'The critical faculty is not self-sustaining. It can only develop on the basis of beliefs which are accepted – in the first instance – uncritically. If the capacity to believe is not developed along with the capacity to criticise, the results can only be fanaticism or nihilism.'

In the same lecture Bishop Newbigin deals cogently with the policy (urged in a British Humanist Association pamphlet[11] and discussed in the Birmingham syllabus) of introducing pupils to a wide range of 'stances for living' without making value judgment about them. He writes:

> 'I am totally unconvinced. There are certainly more racists and hedonists in England than there are Marxists and humanists. The fact is that we do not include these in the syllabus because we know that it would be *wrong* to offer these as stances for living to children – even though we could doubtless find some pretty stories about the personal behaviour of Adolf Hitler at home to go beside those about Lenin in the Birmingham syllabus.'

This is only a brief tour of the RE country. Anyone doing RE should make a careful study of the ground. Everyone going into teaching should have enough general knowledge to help clear the fog which rises whenever the subject gets mentioned.

Assessment

Assessment is an emotive subject. Almost any day's newspaper will reveal someone saying that standards are falling, examinations are too easy or too hard or too often. Most staff rooms contain representatives of all views from those who believe in regular tests to those who would do away with examinations altogether. Beyond the staff room are employers who like certificates, preferably ones they have known for a long time, and higher education with UCCA as its ritual, and A level as its prayer book. Somewhere in between are the examining boards who make up a substantial industry, both home and export (one overseas examining board is the largest single earner of foreign income in its county). In any study you make of examination systems, you will be sure to meet the goings-on of the Schools Council who have striven over the years to make our national system of assessment fit the changing patterns of education. The newly approved 16 + GCSE is the result of eight years' work and has been hailed as bringing sense into 16 + examining, or condemned as recklessly destroying standards. Their ten-year labour over 18 + examining, with Major/Minor, Q & F, and now N & F, is still unfinished.

Even at 18 + the examiners are not done. Indeed, they are just sharpening their instruments for the exams that really sort out the élite from the rest. You yourself are probably painfully aware of the next hurdle looming ahead – unless you belong to an institution which goes in for continuous assessment alone.

All this, of course, is only the tip of the iceberg – the part of assessment that results in official bits of paper. Submerged beneath the educational sea lie masses of assessment, from the five-minute vocabulary test to the mid-year examinations, reports to parents, anguished discussions in staff meetings as to whether Maud should go up or stay in the same set. There are also many assessment activities which do not yield even the scrappy bit of paper used for vocabulary tests – all the impressions a teacher gets of a pupil; the *obiter dicta* of staff-room gossip: 'She's a nice kid, but she can't spell ... you can't believe a word he says ...'.

We all agree ...
Well, nearly all of us. Whatever existentialists say in their more expansive moments, if any of them actually get into a classroom, they quickly join the rest of the teachers who

make judgments about pupils' work. In some subjects answers are either right or wrong; in others things are less sharply drawn but there are criteria to sift better from worse; teachers quickly learn to distinguish original work from dreary copies of reference books. Logicians would point out that the concept of education involves the concept of assessment. There must be something to teach; there must be some way of knowing whether you have taught it and whether it has been learnt.

You may already have noticed that there is less doubt about the possibility of assessment in some subjects than in others. Scientists seem to revel in tests and to mark them with complete assurance. So do language teachers – there's only one way to spell the words (with correct accents) and one way to conjugate the verbs. In history and geography you can get your knuckles rapped for getting facts wrong, but there is more latitude as to what you argue from them. In English, according to some people, you can get away with almost anything as 'your own insight' – though many teachers are reactionary enough to give you a poor mark if your insight goes against all the commentators. However, there is a fair area of agreement. In most schools, most of the time, give or take a spelling correction or two, assessment is acknowledged as an important part of the trade.

There is just one other matter to mention. What has been said so far has referred to *content*, though even there differences begin to appear as we move to the area of values. Wider differences appear when we consider who is doing the work. Does 'good' mean 'worthy of praise by any standard' – or does it mean 'good for Johnny because he hasn't upset any ink over it this time'? Are there different yardsticks for different people? How can we acknowledge the differences in background and opportunity of our pupils, without falling into a morass of relativism and subjectivity?

Why test?

For behaviourists – those interested mainly in a machine

or animal model of human behaviour – tests are useful in two ways. They serve as reinforcement of learning, since the recall in the test and the reward of getting it right impress the material more firmly in the memory – and also make the pupil more likely to go on learning. Tests also act as a valuable monitor on the teaching process. If class A get good marks and class B get worse marks, then we can look into what's happening in Class B in much the same way that an engineer sorts out part of a machine that is not working properly.

At another level, but also looking at society as a machine, testing is the filter by which the next generation are allocated to appropriate roles in society. Examinations are a filter – more or less efficient – to give industry and commerce its labour force in the correct packages.

Both these views have some truth in them, but Christians will not want to let the matter rest there. If this was all there was to it, then schools would be more like factories, or pit-head sieves, than *people*-growing places.

Intuitionists will go further and say it is obvious that pupil's work must be assessed – they may differ a little about whether content, or presentation, or sensitivity, or style should matter most, but some sort of comment must be made. Those who make reason their guide will be more rigid and insist that assessment should be consistent, that different grading must reflect significant, describable difference of performance. They may well want to confine their attention to the pupil's work and regard the pupil's circumstances as irrelevant. On the other hand they may be prepared to take into account differences of background and opportunity, provided a consistent system can be devised that clearly relates to the object of the educative process. Much of the Schools Council's work on assessment has been an attempt to analyse what factors are relevant and what weight should be put upon them in assessment. Throughout the long reports and working papers, there is a welter of evidence and a steady effort to deduce from this what ought to happen.

All these points, and more, you will meet in whatever discussion of assessment features in your course. With much of it Christians will agree, but yet want to add other things. Two main lines of enquiry may be suggested.

Two kinds of testing

You can engage in a fascinating Bible study by looking up references to testing, tempting, trying, and kindred words. There are tests that are good for the people who are tested; tests that show people what they are capable of. One group of words is connected with the goldsmith, who tests and purifies his metal; so Job expresses his desperate hope, 'When he has tried me, I shall come forth as gold' (Jb. 23:10). Another word (*nasah, eg.*, Gn. 22:1; Dt. 8:2) is one for the 'outward bound' enthusiast. The test shows you what you can stand. Abraham's faith was strengthened after it had undergone the traumatic challenge to give up his son. Certainly this idea peeps through some of the tests at school – pupils do get better with suitable testing, and often gain confidence.

But now for the bad news. The Bible also has a number of words for tests that tear down – 'tempt' as the King James version has it. The Pharisees' efforts to 'test' Jesus were not to assess his understanding of Roman tax law, but to make him look a fool in front of the people. You may still find the occasional school teacher who asks all the tricky, twisted questions to catch his class out. It is true that biblical passages are concerned with the testing of character rather than academic achievement, but very often the place and manner of assessment in a school has significance beyond the academic. The brand of failure and the swollen head are moral matters, and so are the effects that follow.

The place of judgment

Ruth Etchells has written[12] of the need to make real the concept of judgment. She argues that teachers must deal with two sorts of knowledge, 'that which we spell out in terms of history, physics, biology at whatever level we teach, and that other kind of knowledge which has to do with the "terrible living world" of good and bad as it is intimately known in each human being.' Here again is the distinction hinted at earlier – between facts and their evaluation. It may well be a mark of our fallenness that we deal more easily with the former but are reluctant to talk as firmly about values; yet the awareness of moral values may well be more real (if more mysterious) to the children we teach than the facts we insist upon so strongly. Indeed, frequently the facts only come to life for anyone when their moral implication becomes frighteningly real. Statistics about immigrant unemployment may be just another boring part of social studies until a black lad sees his older brother decaying for lack of work.

Miss Etchells goes on to point out the teacher's task:

'I suggest we need to make real for the world again the concept of judgment as an inherent component of reality, a part of the way things are. The more I meet and talk with students, the more I listen to some educational theorists, the more I become aware that this reality of judgment is being denied, and that therefore the crucial meeting point between two kinds of knowledge is being avoided ... God meant our knowledge to be in the context of obedience, a recognition of certain laws which are immanent within the universe because they are expressions of the nature of the creator. Real wisdom involves that kind of discrimination. It involves, in fact, judgment. Judgment is such a dirty word at the moment (though it is all right to 'evaluate' as long as you do it creditably!) that we have lost sight of the ground, the essential ground, for discrimination. We have lost sight too of what the full range and glory of the concept of judgment is. This is where teachers have an all important task. It is for us to relate what *we* know of the "terrible living world", within and without, to the wonderful living world of judgment within the grace of God.'

This widens the whole discussion to include judgment to which we are *all* subject. This is not a teacher dispassionately marking a vocabulary test while listening to a favourite record; it is not a mark given out to a pupil by someone who is beyond question, a different sort of Olympian being (clad, in the old days, in a gown to prove his otherness). It is about judgment which is part of the reality of being human. Miss Etchells continues:

> 'The professional relationship can be a killing thing. Unless we understand profoundly that our children, our students, are in the deepest sense potentially our friends, because we share humanness with them, we can never establish for them the truth, the breadth, the grace and the glory of God's judgment as a reality in life ...
> Under that judgment – which is our glory because we are worthy of it, and our disaster because we cannot meet it – stands one of us, representing all of us, who *can* meet it. If we have let Him be our representative, if we agree that He is one with us, if we accept that somehow we are one with Him, then as well as knowing the glory we derive from Him, we have to share as teachers the pain which He derives from us, all of us.'

There is a lot to be done to work out the implications of this biblical view of judgment. Our age has lost any sure basis for discrimination. At one extreme, machine views link everything to cause and result in an inevitability which rules out judgment as a moral reality. The tidy bureaucrat likes to keep things running smoothly, and law becomes a mere instrument of social administration. There is also the strident teacher who is ready to pronounce judgment and condemnation on everyone he teaches (and most of his colleagues) – but with no suggestion of fellow-feeling nor any understanding that there is glory (for his pupils *and himself*) in being worth judging. Christians will have the more demanding task of following him who came not to judge the world but to save, and yet, by his coming, shed his light upon everyone.

Once again, what happens and what ought to happen may be widely different. You will make little impression on the examination industry nationally. You may not make much impression on the assessment system of your own school. But thinking about it is not a waste of time. It may influence how you operate the system, how you run your own classes. It will also mean you will have something thoughtful to contribute if the subject does arise.

1 P. Adams *et al, Children's Rights* (Panther, 1972).
2 ed. N. Bagnal, *Parent Power* (Routledge & Kegan Paul, 1974).
3 P. Adams *et al, Children's Rights, p.* 97.
4 J. P. White, *Towards a Compulsory Curriculum* (Routledge & Kegan Paul, 1973).
5 R. S. Peters, *Ethics and Education* (Allen & Unwin, 1966).
6 B. Palmer, *Spectrum*, Vol. 2 no. 3, 1970.
7 J. Calvin, *Institutes*, II. viii. 1.
8 B. Mitchell, *The Fourth R* (The National Society & SPCK, 1970).
9 E. Hulmes, *Spectrum*, Vol. 11 no. 1, 1979.
10 May and Johnston, *Religion in our Schools* (Hodder & Stoughton, 1968).
11 *Objective, Fair and Balanced* (British Humanist Association, 1977).
12 Ruth Etchells, *Spectrum*, Vol. 9 no. 2, 1977.

Over to you

The few areas picked out in the foregoing pages serve only to show how much more there is to look at, and to look at in much more detail. But I hope what has been said will have made (even laboured) the point that presuppositions matter. What you start with will influence where you end up; what you assume will affect the way you act. Christianity claims to be about the basis and springs of living; it deals in fundamental questions of who we are, why we are here and whose idea it was to have the 'us' and the 'here' in the first place. Because these questions are so basic, they must affect all of life – including educational theory and the day-to-day educational practice that will make up a great part of your life in future. Many of your conclusions will be similar to those of your non-Christian colleagues, but this is only the same as you find in other spheres of living. There is a distinctively Christian view of food (1 Tim. 4:3–5), but once you've given thanks you get working with the knife, fork, spoon or chopsticks in much the same way as folk of other faiths or none. Chalk writes on the blackboard for you all; visual aids work as often for them as for you. Learn about such shared skills and aims, but also, while you have the chance, before the steady pressure of the daily task makes time for thought scarce, start working out what your own special presuppositions as a believing Christian have to say about the job you are starting.